PRA[ctical]
SOCIA[l work]

Series Editor[:] [Jo Campling]

BASW

Editorial Advisory Board:
Robert Adams, Terry Bamford, Charles Barker,
Lena Dominelli, Malcolm Payne, Michael Preston-Shoot,
Daphne Statham and Jane Tunstill

Social work is at an important stage in its development. All professions must be responsive to changing social and economic conditions if they are to meet the needs of those they serve. This series focuses on sound practice and the specific contribution which social workers can make to the well-being of our society.

The British Association of Social Workers has always been conscious of its role in setting guidelines for practice and in seeking to raise professional standards. The conception of the Practical Social Work series arose from a survey of BASW members to discover where they, the practitioners in social work, felt there was the most need for new literature. The response was overwhelming and enthusiastic, and the result is a carefully planned, coherent series of books. The emphasis is firmly on practice set in a theoretical framework. The books will inform, stimulate and promote discussion, thus adding to the further development of skills and high professional standards. All the authors are practitioners and teachers of social work representing a wide variety of experience.

JO CAMPLING

A list of published titles in this series follows overleaf

Practical Social Work
Series Standing Order ISBN 0–333–69347–7

You can receive future titles in this series as they are published by placing a standing order. Please contact your bookseller or, in the case of difficulty, write to us at the address below with your name and address, the title of the series and the ISBN quoted above.

Customer Services Department, Macmillan Distribution Ltd
Houndmills, Basingstoke, Hampshire RG21 6XS, England

PRACTICAL SOCIAL WORK

Robert Adams *Social Work and Empowerment*

David Anderson *Social Work and Mental Handicap*

Sarah Banks *Ethics and Values in Social Work*

James G. Barber *Beyond Casework*

James G. Barber *Social Work with Addictions*

Peter Beresford and Suzy Croft *Citizen Involvement*

Suzy Braye and Michael Preston-Shoot *Practising Social Work Law (2nd edn)*

Helen Cosis Brown *Social Work and Sexuality*

Robert Brown, Stanley Bute and Peter Ford *Social Workers at Risk*

Alan Butler and Colin Pritchard *Social Work and Mental Illness*

Crescy Cannan, Lynne Berry and Karen Lyons *Social Work and Europe*

Roger Clough *Residential Work*

David M. Cooper and David Ball *Social Work and Child Abuse*

Veronica Coulshed *Management in Social Work*

Veronica Coulshed *Social Work Practice (2nd edn)*

Paul Daniel and John Wheeler *Social Work and Local Politics*

Peter R. Day *Sociology in Social Work Practice*

Lena Dominelli *Anti-Racist Social Work (2nd edn)*

Celia Doyle *Working with Abused Children (2nd edn)*

Angela Everitt and Pauline Hardiker *Evaluating for Good Practice*

Angela Everitt, Pauline Hardiker, Jane Littlewood and Audrey Mullender *Applied Research for Better Practice*

Kathy Ford and Alan Jones *Student Supervision in Social Work*

David Francis and Paul Henderson *Working with Rural Communities*

Michael D. A. Freeman *Children, their Families and the Law*

Alison Froggatt *Family Work with Elderly People*

Danya Glaser and Stephen Frosh *Child Sexual Abuse (2nd edn)*

Gill Gorell Barnes *Working with Families*

Cordelia Grimwood and Ruth Popplestone *Women, Management and Care*

Jalna Hanmer and Daphne Statham *Women and Social Work*

Tony Jeffs and Mark Smith (eds) *Youth Work*

Michael Kerfoot and Alan Butler *Problems of Childhood and Adolescence*

Joyce Lishman *Communication in Social Work*

Carol Lupton and Terry Gillespie (eds) *Working with Violence*

Mary Marshall and Mary Dixon *Social Work with Older People (3rd edn)*

Paula Nicolson and Rowan Bayne *Applied Psychology for Social Workers (2nd edn)*

Kieran O'Hagan *Crisis Intervention in Social Services*

Michael Oliver *Social Work with Disabled People*

Joan Orme and Bryan Glastonbury *Care Management*

Malcolm Payne *Working in Teams*

John Pitts *Working with Young Offenders*

Michael Preston-Shoot *Effective Groupwork*

Peter Raynor, David Smith and Maurice Vanstone *Effective Probation Practice*

Steven Shardlow and Mark Doel *Practice Learning and Teaching*

Carole R. Smith *Social Work with the Dying and Bereaved*

David Smith *Criminology for Social Work*

Gill Stewart and John Stewart *Social Work and Housing*

Christine Stones *Focus on Families*

Neil Thompson *Anti-Discriminatory Practice (2nd edn)*

Neil Thompson, Michael Murphy and Steve Stradling *Dealing with Stress*

Derek Tilbury *Working with Mental Illness*

Alan Twelvetrees *Community Work (2nd edn)*

Hilary Walker and Bill Beaumont (eds) *Working with Offenders*

Social Work and Sexuality

Working with Lesbians and Gay Men

Helen Cosis Brown

MACMILLAN

First published 1998 by
MACMILLAN PRESS LTD
Houndmills, Basingstoke, Hampshire RG21 6XS
and London
Companies and representatives
throughout the world

ISBN 0-333-60884-4

A catalogue record for this book is available
from the British Library.

10 9 8 7 6 5 4 3 2 1
07 06 05 04 03 02 01 00 99 98

Copy-edited and typeset by Povey–Edmondson
Tavistock and Rochdale, England

Printed in Hong Kong

This book is written for lesbians and gay men,
both as service users and providers; for a more creative,
celebratory, reflective and competent future.

Contents

Acknowledgements

This book has grown out of the opportunities I have had, since being involved with direct social work delivery, to reflect on my own, and others' practice. I have learnt more from service users and clients than from anyone and I am indebted to their ability to share their thoughts and experiences with me over a number of years.

I have been greatly influenced by and am grateful to my colleagues in practice, particularly to those I learnt a great deal from, including Sue Anderson, Jeanette Brewster, Charlie Burr, Chris Cotter, Barbara Eaton, Ena Fry, Joy Howard, Peter Morgan, Jenny Pearce, Pilly Sharpe, Jane Stacey and Robert Wilson.

My time as a principal lecturer at Middlesex University enabled me to relate my practice experience to a theoretical base. I wish to acknowledge the input of the following to that process: Anthony Borgiono, Elaine Creith, Jane Dutton, Tony Goodman, MaryAnn Henderson, Ravi Kohli, Michele McCarthy, Cathy McGowen, Jenny Pearce, Phil Slater, and the many lesbian and gay students who helped me deconstruct and reconstruct some of my ideas.

The writing, collating and production of the book has been facilitated by inputs from firstly, Diane Adderley (who proof read and typed the first draft), Kate Jarvis, Dawn Sharpe and my very patient and supportive editor, Jo Campling, and the helpful contribution of my two anonymous readers.

My thanks go to the following organisations and individuals who were generous with their thoughts, materials, information and guidance: The Albert Kennedy Trust, All Saints Bookshop (Middlesex University), Angie Mason and Stonewall, Anthea Lowe of the Anti-discrimination Board of New South Wales, AUT (Association of University Teachers), GALOP (Gay London Policing Group), Gays the Word, NAPO (National Association of Probation Officers), NATFHE (National Association of Teachers in Further and Higher Education), Rights of Women Lesbian Custody Group and UNISON.

Underpinning the over-long completion of this project has been the support of my friends and children. My gratitude is due to Aaron Brown, Julian Lousada, Clare Parkinson, Jo Rosenthal, Casey Ryan, Clare Widgery and Elaine Creith, who at the end gave invaluable practical and intellectual support.   HELEN COSIS BROWN

1

Introduction

This book is premised upon two assumptions. The first is that lesbians and gay men constitute two separate but linked, oppressed groups; the second, that it is possible for social work to deliver a competent non-oppressive practice to individuals and communities within those groups. The oppression of lesbians and gay men is made concrete through discriminatory legislation that impacts on them directly, and by individual, group and institutional prejudice against them and physical assault. The social control of lesbians and gay men is a powerful external force affecting individuals' life chances and potential, and equally importantly impacts on individuals' sense of themselves in relation to others and society. Lesbians and gay men can identify with or internalise prejudicial ideas about homosexuality, which has a significant affect on how they live their lives, how they relate to others and how they perceive themselves. The majority of lesbians and gay men find external and internal processes and resources to manage this oppression, but for some this is not the case. Social work, by its unique contribution of focusing on the individual and the social, can make a significant contribution by facilitating the development and utilisation of such internal and external processes and resources, to enable these to develop where they either did not exist or were lying dormant.

Historically, social work has contributed to the oppression of lesbians and gay men both at an individual and collective level. As a profession it has added to and propagated ideas pathologising homosexuality. Social work is subject to contradictions and is not a homogeneous entity but a collection of dynamic individuals, organisations and ideas, many of which have delivered a competent service to lesbians and gay men. Lesbians and gay men are not a homogeneous group either, but are made up of equally diverse individuals, organisations, groups, communities and ideas. In this book I refer, in the main, to lesbian and gay communities (plural),

1

rather than community (singular), the better to reflect the degree of
that diversity. The book is concerned with social work with people
who identify or are identified as lesbian and gay, not with homosexual acts. Many heterosexuals engage in homosexual acts but
neither perceive themselves nor are perceived by others as lesbian or
gay. I am concerned with homosexuality as an identity not as a
sexual practice, although the two very often go together, and in
separating them out I am not denying the importance of sex.

Conversation

Beliefs need to be made explicit, as they often underpin ideas in
social work theory, and behaviours in practice. A central belief
underpinning this book is that change is possible at an individual,
group, organisational, community and societal level. Even where
change is not achieved, the belief in its possibility affects the people
concerned. As individuals we function in different capacities: as
social worker, parent, lover, trade unionist, political activist. As
individuals engaged in trying to bring about change in relation to an
area of oppression – in this case oppression affecting lesbians and
gay men – we have to target our activities in relevant and appropriate ways that are the most likely to facilitate change. This book is
concerned with the interrelationship between, on the one hand,
social workers, social work ideas, social work organisations and
social work practice, and, on the other hand, lesbians and gay men.
The possibility of change within these interrelationships will be
specific and will not lead to the 'liberation' of lesbians and gay
men, but rather will be small and incremental, slowly eroding
oppressive attitudes and behaviours.

Change is something that is facilitated. Forced change rarely lasts.
Some changes have to be forced; social work is engaged in both the
facilitation of change and its enforcement. Attitudinal changes have
to be facilitated, but behavioural changes can be enforced. We can
produce procedures to prevent harassment of lesbian and gay
workers that control behaviours, but cannot prevent people holding
prejudiced ideas. In the arena of anti-oppressive practice this is a
complex interrelationship. There is not a clear-cut relationship
between belief and behaviour, although changing behaviour can
affect beliefs. However, it is behaviours that impact on others, and I

am including communication within behaviours. In the social work context the individual behaviours of social workers have had as much impact on lesbians and gay men as organisational ideologies.

To engage in change there needs to be dialogue, conversation. Conversation assumes an equality of engagement, the possibility of exchange, listening and contributing. Engaging in conversation is an essential component of the development of anti-oppressive practice. Anti-oppressive practice is about the breaking of new ground, entering unfamiliar spaces, where we need to move with some degree of hesitancy and humility because it is other people's lives we affect in this process. Rhetoric and retribution have little place within conversation and the development of anti-oppressive practice but, understandably, they featured in the early debates and discussions, as part of a process of being heard, to catch the attention of those who were perceived as holding power. The attention has been caught and we are now able to enter the realms of complexity and the engagement with contradictions.

Language

Language has been problematic in the development of anti-oppressive practice. The newness of the ideas and the practice developments have sometimes led to a language of certainty. In the period when anti-oppressive practice was still off the agendas of both the agency and the academy, the battles to put anti-oppressive practice onto those agendas were inevitably littered with attacking and defensive debates, with little room for the languages of ambivalence and ambiguity. However, today anti-oppressive ideas and practices are developmentally in a more advanced and secure stage, and there can now be an appreciation that in the development of new ideas there needs to be reflection and caution.

A problematic use of language has been the absorption of terms that originated out of social and political resistance into mainstream discourse. The terms homophobia and heterosexism are now in standard use. They are used as if they describe some simple, factual, concrete reality, rather than trying to grapple with the complexities of perceptions, beliefs, actions, policies and statutes that make up the movable, sometimes intangible, but always powerful oppression of lesbians and gay men. In fact, these terms have been used in ways that are reductionist and shorthand, and have been difficult to translate back into their full richness. Of course, we sometimes need to use shorthand and I make no apology for using such terms throughout this book. The reader is asked to accept that I appreciate that their use is problematic and that subsumed within them are a complex set of interrelationships and experiences that will change and evolve. Stewart gives a useful summary of generally accepted and understood meanings. The term heterosexism developed from the 1970s Gay Liberation Movement's use of the term heterocentrism. Heterosexism is described as:

> term for prejudice against lesbians and gay men . . . Its relation to the concept homophobia is similar to the relationship between sexism and misogyny; that is, the relation is simply a question of degree. Both heterosexism and homophobia form part of the same continuum of anti-gay feeling, and are built upon the belief that heterosexuality is somehow inherently normal and superior. (Stewart, 1995: 116).

Stewart defines homophobia as 'the fear or hatred of homosexuals, [it] is colloquially used as the word for beliefs which explicitly or implicitly put down lesbians and gay men' (1995: 121). There has been much debate about the usefulness of the term homophobia, as it assumes a degree of irrational behaviour guided by the unconscious, whereas many gay activists would stress the rational, intended oppression of lesbians and gay men that is not just located in the realms of the unconscious.

Another shorthand adopted in this book is the use of 'Britain'. Britain covers different countries with different nationalities, languages, cultures and histories. Because of these differences, the lives and circumstances of lesbians and gay men, for example, in different countries within Britain will vary (Crwydren, 1994; Boyd *et al.*, 1986), and so will the ways they are perceived and perceive themselves.

Structure

Alongside the growth of ideas relating to the debates around the development of anti-oppressive practice, a body of literature has grown up. A glaring omission from the literature in the British context until 1996 (Logan *et al.*, 1996), but not in the American, were texts written in the last ten years that specifically addressed the relationship between social work and lesbian and gay communities. This is, after all, the period within which the production of anti-oppressive social work practice materials has been comparatively prolific.

This book is a contribution to the beginning of trying to fill that gap. It offers an overview of social work with lesbians and gay men. Because of the nature of overviews, some areas (for example, drug use, domestic violence in same-sex relationships and juvenile justice) are not covered. I have drawn on areas where I have direct practice experience as well as a theoretical understanding. It is one contribution towards a conversation about social work with lesbians and gay men. It is also one person's perspective, drawing on existing relevant and related written materials, on my own experience as a social worker and team leader within a local authority social work department, and as a social work lecturer, and, importantly, on conversations with clients and/or service users, students and colleagues.

The book is structured in such a way so as to build on relevant knowledge chapter by chapter. Although each chapter can be taken separately, there is an assumption that the material from previous chapters will have been covered. The book progresses from the general to the more specific. This is done in the belief that it is important to contextualise social work practice with lesbians and gay men in its detailed form, within a broader framework, thus enabling there to be a more thorough understanding of dynamics and dilemmas that have and still do impact on this area of practice. The said broader framework includes such areas as notions of competent practice, anti-discriminatory practice, and the social–political context surrounding lesbians and gay men both as social workers and as service users and clients. This contextualisation of social work practice with lesbians and gay men needs to happen prior to discussions of specific practice issues and areas of practice. The aim of the book is to build on the competences of students, social workers, managers and social work teachers, by contributing additional knowledge, ideas and reflections to consider when working with lesbians and gay men.

Chapter 2 explores the usefulness of the concept of competence as a starting point, by examining its components of social work knowledge, values and skills, and examining some of its contradictions and its potential usefulness in the delivery of anti-oppressive practice, to lesbians and gay men clients and service users. Chapter 3 locates the oppression of lesbians and gay men, and the relationship of social work to this oppression, within its wider political and social context. This happens at the beginning of the book to enable the reader to locate and anchor social work developments in this area within a wider social and political context. Two legislative contexts are surveyed and compared – those of New South Wales, Australia, and of Britain: one with protective legislation for lesbians and gay men and one without it. The question is considered of whether or not the presence or absence of such legislation affects the respective lesbian and gay social workers and service users and clients within those countries.

Lesbian and gay workers have often found themselves to be problematised within their respective professions, having their sexuality becoming the focus of an employing agency's or supervisor's attentions, rather than their professional competence. This subject is explored in Chapter 4, as are the issues around coming out, and the different realities and experiences of Black lesbians and gay men in this process. Social work education is also covered within this chapter. There is no clear relationship between the experiences of lesbian and gay social workers as a group and those of lesbians and gay service users and clients, indeed there are significant differences including their respective relationships to power in the social work context. However, the degree of confidence and security experienced by lesbians and gay social workers within their agencies is likely to impact on the quality of service provision delivered by those agencies to lesbian and gay individuals and communities. Social work education is also covered within the same chapter. Leading on from that, a crucial aspect of the educational process of social work is the imparting of knowledge that is relevant to social work practice. Because this knowledge is such a vast entity, it is covered under three headings, namely:

knowledge that informs the practitioner about the client's experience and context; knowledge that helps the practitioner plan appropriate intervention; and knowledge that clarifies the practi-

tioner's understanding of the legal, policy, procedural and organisational context in which their practice takes place. (Brown
1996: 10)

Chapter 5 looks at the problematic nature of social work knowledge
as it has been applied to lesbians and gay men. I argue that the use
of knowledge has to be critically evaluated and new knowledge
sought out, while remaining wary that we don't 'throw the baby out
with the bath water'. We should, rather, be re-evaluating knowledge
by placing it within its cultural, economic, historical and geographical context. We may then be able to re-examine its relevance to
lesbian and gay experience.

Social work takes place within specific organisational contexts.
Chapter 6 examines generic matters relevant to all organisations and
contexts that are likely to dictate the quality of service delivered to
lesbians and gay men. Chapters 2 to 6 lay the foundation for
Chapters 7 to 9, setting the context in which the following chapters,
which each concentrate on an area of practice, can be explored.
Each of these following chapters relates to the organisation of social
work practice at the point of delivery, which is increasingly the
'norm', of organising both assessment and provision around client/
service user groups who are the focus of specific pieces of legislation.
Chapter 7 looks at social work with children and families, Chapter 8
focuses on social work with adults, and Chapter 9 deals with social
work and probation practice with offenders. These three chapters
take, as their focus, considerations in relation to lesbians and gay
men as clients/service users.

'The social worker is one primary resource available to the client.
The resources that workers can provide are based on the professional knowledge, values, and skills they possess' (Pierce, 1992: 175).
The available knowledge that is relevant to social work with lesbians
and gay men has been limited; this book is offered as one contribution to the knowledge base on which social workers may discrimi-
natingly draw.

2

Competent Anti-Discriminatory Social Work Practice

The concept of competence in social work

Competence has been a buzz-word in social work education and practice in the recent past, and is still in current use. Both as a term and as an organising principle it held so much sway that it became the structuring focus for the British social work qualification, the Diploma in Social Work (DipSW) (CCETSW, 1989; CCETSW, 1995). Interestingly, given the general acceptance of the usefulness of competence as an organising principle within both practice and education, there has been little explicit discussion of either what is meant by the word within the social work context, or whether or not its application to social work practice will be of benefit to social work clients and service users. Given this lack of clarity, it is necessary to state what is meant by the term as it is used in this book. It is beyond the scope of the book to enter into a complex discussion about the concept of competence, its origins and use in social work. However, it is relevant to briefly examine the idea as it pertains to social work with lesbians and gay men.

In this context, competence means simply to be able to practise adequately in the interests of clients and service users. However, things are not quite so simple. There has been little agreement on what constitutes social work practice, let alone what is competent practice. More is known about what constitutes incompetent practice, and, within the area of childcare this has been fully explored and documented (Department of Health, 1991a). It was within the area of childcare that some of the seeds of the dominance of the idea of competence within social work education and practice were sown.

8

The Beckford inquiry (London Borough of Brent, 1985) emphasised the need for social work education to be reviewed, in the light of the inquiry's findings. It seemed, not unreasonably, that it was pertinent that social workers should be equipped to know what they were meant to be doing and how and why they were meant to do it. They were also expected, through the educational process, to be enabled to account for their particular activity within the legislative framework from which social work's powers and duties were drawn. The resulting changes in British social work education were established in the Diploma in Social Work (CCETSW, 1989; CCETSW, 1991; CCETSW, 1995).

In these documents, it can be argued, CCETSW saw a competent practitioner as one who, for every activity they were engaged in, sought out applicable knowledge to inform their intervention, thought through the values and value dilemmas that might be relevant to the activity, and, lastly, had the appropriate skills to accomplish the tasks that were involved in completing the activity. For the purposes of this book, this would seem a helpful way of defining a competent practitioner. It is to be hoped that while the purpose of this endeavour is to focus on competent social work practice with lesbians and gay men, it may also throw light on how such a seemingly straightforward desire as that for social workers to be competent is in reality complex and fraught with contradictions.

CCETSW did not pioneer the emphasising of outcomes in social work practice, or focusing on the knowledge, values and skills to be employed by practitioners; many influential texts had similar emphasis (Younghusband, 1959; CCETSW, 1975; Barclay, 1982). In its role of redefining the tasks for social work education, CCETSW echoed several themes within the Barclay report. The report argued that there should be an emphasis on defining the roles and tasks of social work, trying to define more clearly what social workers actually do: 'it is by concentrating on these activities that we think the skills and knowledge that will be helpful to social workers can most readily be identified' (Barclay, 1982: 151).

Recent British legislation and Government directives have been concerned to make sure that social workers are competent and effective. The Mental Health Act 1983, when discussing the appointment of approved social workers (ASWs), requires the local authority to ensure that they have the '. . . appropriate competence in dealing with persons who are suffering from mental disorder' (Jones,

1994: 168). The White Paper on community care reflected similar concerns, pointing out the need for qualifying training for social workers to equip them to operate effectively in their new roles (Department of Health, 1989). Competent and effective practice is not just a desirable idea; it is a requirement enshrined in legislation, so it would seem that it may well be a useful focus when thinking about practice with lesbians and gay men.

Competence: knowledge, values and skills; strengths and dilemmas

The examination of social work with lesbians and gay men, historically, tells us a lot about incompetent practice (Hart and Richardson, 1981; Kus, 1990a; Brown, 1992a). The evidence suggests that the oppression that lesbians and gay men experience generally in society is also reflected in their experiences as social work clients/service users: 'Heterosexism is a deeply ingrained set of ideas and practices both within and outside social work' (Thompson, 1993: 135). There would, not surprisingly, seem to be a link here between oppression, discrimination and incompetent practice. However, rather than leaving such a statement as a truism that would result in little more than ideological posturing, it is important that we try to have some idea as to why this might be the case. After all, practitioners endeavouring to practise in the best interests of their clients are not some new species that has evolved since the onset of discussions about competence; where practitioners have been identified as misguided or incompetent, we can generally assume their intentions were benevolent. Why, then, has social work so often failed in delivering a competent service to lesbians and gay men, and why have some social work interventions been experienced by lesbians and gay men as malevolent? The answer to this question is complex; this book is intended to unravel aspects of that complexity, but that unravelling will inevitably be incomplete. Initially it may be helpful to look at some of the dilemmas involved with the use of this organising concept of competence.

One of the major difficulties with the term is that it means very different things to different people (Brandon and Davis, 1979; O'Hagan, 1996). A consequence of these varied interpretations of meaning may add to, rather than subtract from, the confusion surrounding what 'good enough' social work might consist of.

Another criticism of the emphasis on competence has been its potentially mechanistic impact on social work practice, leading to the development of a simplistic, procedural response to what are very complex human dilemmas, which rarely have straightforward solutions. The fear is the creation of the practitioner who methodically follows their agency's procedures manual, irrespective of the specific and unique circumstances of a given situation: a worker who is unable to use their own professional judgement. Howe writes that

> making social work a technical pursuit in which methods and techniques are emphasised at the expense of the moral component, causes it to look inwards. It cuts its ties with society. All it can offer is a technical service to those who are interested. (Howe, 1979: 40).

Let us take the definition of a competent practitioner used earlier in this chapter: one who, for every activity they undertake, seeks out applicable knowledge to inform their actions, thinks through the values and value dilemmas that are relevant to the activity and ensures that they have the appropriate skills to accomplish the tasks that are involved in completing the activity. By breaking down this definition into its component parts of knowledge, values and skills, and examining each component separately, we may more easily be able to address the issue of what constitutes adequate practice, as well as being able to illuminate why practice with lesbians and gay men has sometimes been woefully inadequate.

Knowledge

The relationship between knowledge and practice has been and continues to be problematic. We emphasise the importance of linking theory and practice, indeed we make the ability to integrate the two, and the ability to articulate the integration, a requirement for qualification as a professional social worker. We ask a lot, as it has been argued that the 'insistence that theory and practice are complementary aspects of the same thing is part of a verbal rather than a real tradition in social work' (Sheldon, 1978: 1). Other research showed that few social workers informed their work with theory, but were more likely to rely on their own experience or advice from colleagues (Carew, 1979). Sheldon showed there to be two distinct subcultures within social work: a theoretical one and a practical one. The findings of the research undertaken by the research subculture were either 'not "believed", by the practice subculture, or they are seen as the products of a process which has little direct relevance to the practice situation' (Sheldon, 1978: 2). At best we can say the relationship between knowledge and practice is an ambivalent one.

It would also seem that social work, rather than informing its practice with a relevant theoretical base, has sought out knowledge to justify its practice (Brown, 1992b; Brown, 1996).

Knowledge has been highly problematic in its application for methodological reasons. Research findings derived from, or ideas arising out of, specific social and cultural contexts from a particular historical period have often been seen as having universal applicability. Those individuals and communities that did not conform to those universal truths were often pathologised, lesbians and gay men being a case in point. Social work has been slow to critically examine its use of theory in a way that assesses its relevance and usefulness to all its service users. This critical revaluation of social work knowledge is a cornerstone of the development of antidiscriminatory practice. The relationship between social work practice and knowledge is anything but straightforward, the relationship being complex, problematic and ambivalent: familiar dynamics for social workers.

Values

When we turn to values and their relationship to competent practice, we are entering a quagmire. The arena of values and morals is the stuff of daily social work practice. Social work literature reflects the importance of values to practice; it also demonstrates the intense difficulty of this area (Pearce, 1996). There have been, among many others, two fundamental assumptions within the traditional debates about social work values that have particular relevance for lesbians and gay men, and which are interconnected and have often been mirrored in practice. The first is the argument that social work values can be identified, articulated and have universal permanent applicability. This has been a powerful argument which has, until recently, been assumed as a social work 'truth'. The second is that social work values that can be identified and articulated are relevant to all service users, and, as a consequence, all service users are in receipt of an equivalently competent service. These assumptions were dismantled first by the radical social work literature (Statham, 1978; Brake and Bailey, 1980) and then taken further apart by the extensively documented failure of social work to meet the needs of all service users or work effectively with them, documented by the ever increasing anti-discriminatory practice literature, much of which stands as a testament to some of social work's failings (Dominelli, 1988; Dominelli and McLeod, 1989; Hutchinson-Reis, 1989; Ahmad, 1990; Husband, 1991; Oliver, 1991; Brown, 1992a; Langan and Day, 1992; Thompson, 1993).

During the process of social work theoreticians trying to identify and articulate universal values, some of the seeds were being sown from which incompetent practice with lesbians and gay men grew. For example, Biestek, who is often viewed as one of the founding fathers of social work values, made a valiant attempt in trying to identify key areas with his principles of individuation, purposeful expression of feelings, controlled emotional involvement, acceptance, non-judgemental attitude, client self-determination and confidentiality (Biestek, 1957: 17). This would seem a worthwhile and straightforward task, one that would benefit lesbian and gay clients along with everybody else. However, on examining the qualifications made to these seven principles, bringing benefits to lesbians and gay men may not have been the intention. The following quotes are revealing as to some of the limits of social work's generosity in relation to values:

> It is the responsibility of the profession to see that acceptance of the person does not become confused with acceptance of immoral or anti-social deeds. (McKenney, 1951: 28)

> Acceptance does not mean approval of deviant attitudes or behaviour. (Biestek, 1957: 72)

> The non-judgmental attitude in social work is not only compatible with objective norms in human behaviour but actually requires them. (Biestek, 1957: 89)

When these two authors were writing, in Britain and North America, male homosexual acts were not just seen as immoral,

abnormal and deviant: in Britain they were illegal. Lesbians and gay
men were unlikely to reap the benefits of some of Biestek's principles. It has been argued that the principle of 'respect for persons' is
qualified or denied when there is a persistent wilful refusal to act
morally, or when the person's actions break the law (Clark and
Asquith, 1985: 30). Lesbians and gay men were, and still are to a
lesser extent, seen as immoral. Before 1967, sexually active gay men
in Britain were breaking the law. In some circumstances this is still
the case, while lesbian sexual activity remains outside the legal
framework (this will be looked at in Chapter 3). The interface
between social work values and/or principles and homosexuality
illustrates how social work is part of the society in which it operates
and will 'mirror complexities and confusions of thought and action
in society' (CCETSW, 1976: 18). The radical social work tradition
has been invaluable in exposing the complexity of any discussion of
values and their relationship with political, economic and ideological dynamics: 'the place of ideology cannot be ignored in the
formulation or implementation of values. Both have played a large
part in maintaining the status quo' (Statham, 1978: 36).

Political, economic and ideological dynamics have changed in the
last thirty years. This can be traced in the relationship between social
work values and lesbian and gay men. The British Association of
Social Work (BASW) and the Central Council for Education and
Training in Social Work (CCETSW), both now include sexual
orientation in their discussions. BASW and CCETSW both include
sexual orientation in key documents. In BASW's 'principles of social
work practice', one section reads: No prejudice in self, nor tolerance
of prejudice or prejudice in others, on grounds of origin, race, status,
sex, sexual-orientation, age, disability, beliefs or contribution to
society. (BASW, 1988).

CCETSW in 1986 approved the following equal opportunities
policy:

> CCETSW will seek to ensure that in all dimensions of its activity
> as an employer, validating body and its development work,
> individuals are not unfairly disadvantaged on the grounds of
> age, gender, disability, language (including sign language), race,
> ethnic origin, nationality, sexual-orientation, social class or reli-
> gion. (CCETSW, 1986: 1).

The tone of the BASW principle reflects the period in which it was written and as a consequence reads as rather dogmatic and slightly idealistic, but it is a useful illustration of the feelings and quality of the political debates during that period. However, these directives by two powerful organisations may have lulled lesbians and gay men into a false sense of security; the reality has been that many local authorities and voluntary organisations have had great difficulty in accepting the directives. Although the political and social contexts of the discourses surrounding homosexuality have altered considerably since Biestek was drawing up his list of principles, there remains a complex, problematic and ambivalent relationship between social work values and lesbians and gay men.

Skills

Social work skills are often perceived as somehow neutral. This has been refuted by the literature (d'Ardenne and Mahtani, 1989; Munro *et al.*, 1989; Pederson *et al.*, 1989; Dutton and Kohli, 1996). Munro *et al.* look at the significance of power in the dialogue between the helped and the helper. They argue that the helper has to take into account the impact of power on the relationship and the work that is undertaken. They go on to say that this 'inherent inequality in the relationship is usually enlarged when there are ethnic, gender, or other important differences between the counsellor and the client' (Munro *et al.*, 1989: 11). When lesbians and gay men are seeking help, there are often going to be those 'other important differences'.

A number of core skills have been identified, relevant to social work, that can be grouped under five headings: cognitive skills, interpersonal skills, decision making skills, administrative skills, and skills involved in the ability to mobilise resources (CCETSW, 1991: 16). Some of these will be addressed in later chapters, but here we will focus on one aspect – interpersonal skills. If we take one highly influential text, *The Skilled Helper* (Egan, 1990), which carefully examines the micro level of interpersonal interaction to facilitate effective professional helping, we find that there needs to be some sensitive thinking when looking at its application to working with lesbians and gay men. For example, it may be important to lay particular stress on the skills of engagement, listening, the use of probes and empathy, to help establish enough trust to work effectively. Given social work's history of working with lesbians and gay men (see Chapter 3), there will understandably be, for some people, a wariness about engaging in a helping relationship. The consideration of such things as the use of probes in an interview would need to be kept in mind. When working with people who have been, or who are being, discriminated against, the over-use of closed and direct questions can be experienced as persecutory (Finlay and Reynolds, 1987). If we are successfully going to facilitate someone 'telling us their story', then we have to convey to them that we are wanting to hear it in all its complexity, not just a censored version.

The ability to engage with a client involves a particularly important set of skills given the increasing emphasis on assessment. Community care has necessitated a sharpening of skills when undertaking assessments. The ability to establish a relationship of trust, warmth and integrity is central to the process of effective intervention:

> the practitioner has to establish a relationship of trust with potential users and carers; the more personal the needs, the more important is that trust. In order to appreciate needs from the perspective of users themselves, assessors have to rid themselves, as far as possible, of their own prejudices. The tasks of listening, observing and understanding place great demands on staff assessment involves considerable skill in interpersonal relations. (Department of Health, 1991b: 52)

To be able to work effectively also involves being able to work with the uniqueness of each individual within their own context. This requires the bringing together of knowledge, values and skills that will facilitate competent intervention, in the client/service user's interests.

Non-discriminatory perspectives and competent practice

There has been, within social work, a dominant assumption, that 'good' social work practice would be 'good' practice for all clients, irrespective of their structural position within society and of their community's historical relationship with the central and local state.

In practice, this would have meant that if three women – one Black, African-Caribbean woman, in her thirties, and two White English women, one in her thirties and one in her eighties – were referred to a social work office seeking help for depression, the expectation in many areas of social work would have been that they would receive a similar service. The experience of such women and the literature supporting their experience (Brook and Davis, 1985; Langan and Day, 1992) has refuted that assumption. The challenging of firmly held convictions about the universal applicability and the beneficial nature of social work to all clients and service users was a deeply shocking process for many practitioners. Although it would be true that for some practitioners there would have been a conscious dynamic of overtly oppressing and discriminating against clients as a means of bolstering their own power, for most social workers that simply was not the case. The interrelationship between the state, institutional and individual oppression, and how they impact on individual practitioners in particular settings and how this affects their intervention with clients is an enormously complex relationship. Scapegoating and blaming the practitioner for their oppression of clients would be over-simplistic, unhelpful and, in the long term, would not benefit the client/service user.

Returning to the three hypothetical depressed women arriving at the social work agency seeking help, historically the chances are that only the younger white woman would have arrived at the agency at all. The Black, African-Caribbean woman may well have assumed, from experiences of other welfare agencies she may have encountered, that she would come up against what is often referred to as institutional racism as well as individual racism, and that the services which might be offered to her would be designed for others and not for her. The older, white English woman, if she had researched the matter beforehand (Finch and Groves, 1985; Hughes and Mtezuka, 1992), would have known that ageism is so deeply ingrained into some aspects of White British culture, and then reflected in welfare agencies' definitions of and responses to need, that the chances of getting a service at all would be so unlikely that she would be better off staying at home and saving her bus fare.

For the social worker within the hypothetical agency awaiting the arrival of these three women, her intervention would be affected by the political, social, ideological and economic, national and local context in which she was located. Her intervention would also be affected by who she was, her own relationship to structural power and oppression, her own community or communities' experience and history, her family or group experience and history and her own unique experience and history and how she had herself processed and made sense of all the above. This social worker would also have been through a social work education process, which she would have been affected by and had very little control over. All these factors would be part of dictating the quality of service that the three women would receive, and that the social worker would be able to offer. The quality of the service a client or service user gets, and whether or not it is experienced as oppressive or not, is dictated by more than the individual attitudes and beliefs of individual workers.

The last twenty years has been a traumatic period for social work, a period in which basic tenets have been dismantled. One of the most painful areas has been the eventual acceptance by the profession that it has not offered an equal service to all service users: that its provision has not only been discriminatory – it has also been oppressive. It was generally accepted that there needed to be an active integration of anti-discriminatory and anti-oppressive perspectives into all aspects of policy and practice for the balance to begin to be redressed. Social work with lesbians and gay men has been one of the last areas to be fully analysed and rethought. It is telling that there are still few publications addressing the area. It is also illuminating that an excellent general text on anti-discriminatory practice devotes only four sides of print to the topic, subsumed under a chapter heading of 'other sources of oppression' (Thompson, 1993). 'Other sources of oppression' has often been the tokenistic and rather anxious approach to rethinking, or indeed thinking at all, about service delivery to lesbians and gay men. The debates and developing literature on anti-discriminatory practice have been part of a complex momentum that has contributed to opening up this area. However, both academics and practitioners can feel criticised in this process, with consequent feelings of anxiety and defensiveness rather than a more helpful analysis.

Competence and anti-discriminatory practice

Focusing on competence as an organising principle within social work practice and education can diffuse some of the unproductive tension generated around this area. If we break competence down into the three components of knowledge, values and skills in the following way, it can contribute to enabling a more manageable understanding:

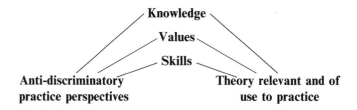

Anti-discriminatory   Theory relevant and of
practice perspectives   use to practice

A competent practitioner would be one who would, for every piece of work they undertake, draw on the following:

1. *The knowledge needed for the particular piece of work.* This comprises, first, knowledge that informs the practitioner about the client/service user's experience and context; second, knowledge that informs the practitioner about the most effective interventions to make; and, third, knowledge of the legal, policy and procedural context that the practice takes place within (Brown, 1996) – see the discussion in Chapter 4. The knowledge base of social work has sometimes been assumed to be somehow neutral, values being the real area where debates around anti-discriminatory practice should be, and often were, located. However, knowledge informing social work practice is no more and no less than research and ideas generated by individuals who are located in a specific political, economic, historical and cultural moment. Knowledge is never neutral. It must always be located within the particular discourses of its time to be of any use to practitioners. The contextualisation of knowledge should be part of what practitioners automatically do before applying it to their practice. Unfortunately this does not always happen. Instead, knowledge is sometimes looked at as neutral and universally applicable, or it is not placed in its own context and dismissed in total, thereby 'throwing out the baby with the bath water', as one aspect of it is perceived as oppressive to someone. A reflective practitioner is one who seeks out relevant knowledge, places that knowledge within its own context and the discourses of the time of its origin, and then assesses its

applicability to a given situation. For lesbian and gay male service users this is essential to the receipt of a relevant and appropriate service.

2. *Values as an aspect of competence.* I would argue that values need to be considered at four levels by the practitioner as they undertake each piece of work: first, the values of the service user/client in relation to a particular piece of work; second, the values of the social worker in relation to the same work; third, the values of the agency in relation to the work; and last, the values enshrined in the policies and legislative context in which the piece of work is being undertaken. How do these four levels of values coincide and how do they differ? Work with lesbians and gay men necessitates the explicit consideration of these four aspects of values by practitioners. Values often conflict, as will be explored, particularly as has been demonstrated when agencies come to consider applications from lesbian and gay men to become foster or adoptive parents (Chapter 7).

3. *Skills.* These, like knowledge, are often perceived as existing outside prejudiced discourses. This is simply not the case (d'Ardenne and Mahtani, 1989; Munro *et al.*, 1989; Dutton and Kohli, 1996). The application of skills must be a discriminatory process, meaning that we discriminate between different situations and different people and see that the application of particular interviewing skills, for example, may be appropriate in one situation with one individual but not with another (Finlay and Reynolds, 1987). Individuals who have experienced considerable discrimination and oppression may need much more work around engagement, to enable the development of trust. The whole complex area of 'coming out' means that some lesbians and gay men are experienced by social workers as being elusive, only telling them half the story, when in fact the client/ service user may need some time to be open about their lives, fearing a negative, embarrassed or hostile response. Social workers may need to apply discrimination in the application of different skills to really offer an anti-discriminatory service.

An effective, competent practitioner, then, is one who thinks critically about their own intervention and their use and application of knowledge, values and skills, this being integral to the development of an anti-discriminatory practice, that is, a practice that

respects the unique specificity of each individual. S
benefit to all service users and is essential for lesb⁻

Power, oppression and empowerment

Anti-discriminatory practice can be considered under two headings. First come the questions pertaining to service delivery to traditionally oppressed groups. Such groups could include older people, disabled people, Black communities, people with learning disabilities, working-class communities, lesbians and gay men, women – the list could go on and on, and would differ according to the compiler's own perspectives. Under this heading, there would be consideration of the historical and socio-political contexts and realities of each group and social work's interrelationship with these. Second comes the consideration of general principles that are relevant to all clients and service users, irrespective of their individual relationship to power. These would include such concepts as empowerment, citizenship, partnership, and user involvement. The development of anti-discriminatory practice literature is reflecting the move towards development in this second area (Dalrymple and Burke, 1995). and the concepts involved have become so accepted that they are often enshrined in legislation and are the currency of both the left and the right wing of political debate (Adams, 1990; Beresford and Croft, 1993; Baistow, 1995). The Children Act 1989 talks of working in partnership and the National Health Service and Community Care Act 1990 brings in its wake Social Services Inspectorate publications that emphasise the importance of empowerment of service users (Smale *et al.*, 1993). Social work delivery to lesbians and gay men necessitates the consideration of anti-discriminatory social work practice under both the above headings. There does need to be an awareness of the specific impacts of heterosexism and homophobia on both the communities of lesbians and gay men and also on the individuals involved. Lesbians and gay men as service users will also benefit the same as all service users from a general commitment to such principles as user involvement and partnership. Competent practice would incorporate the consideration of both these aspects of anti-discriminatory practice in all its activities.

Competent practice with lesbians and gay men

It has been argued that incompetent practice is the result of simple ignorance:

> the vast majority of instances of poor quality care given to gay and lesbian clients is the result of a lack of knowledge on the part of the helping professional, rather than any deep seated homophobia. (Kus, 1990a: 7)

Others have argued that it may be more than ignorance:

> Heterosexism is a deeply ingrained set of ideas and practices both within and outside social work. It is a significant and widespread form of oppression which merits inclusion on the anti-discriminatory practice agenda. (Thompson, 1993: 135)

The complex reality may lie somewhere between these two positions. Certainly the acquisition of knowledge, sadly, does not necessarily lead to the death of prejudice or indeed of incompetence. Rather the relationship between values and knowledge is so entwined that both have to be addressed together for there to be any hope of competence emerging from beneath the undergrowth. For there to be a good enough service delivery to lesbians and gay men, the three areas of knowledge, values and skills need to be considered both together and separately. Simultaneously, anti-discriminatory practice has to be integrated into considerations of the relevant knowledge, values and skills that make up the potential of competent practice.

3

Placing the Debate within its Social/Political Context

The reasons why, historically, anti-discriminatory practice became an acceptable discourse within social work practice in the 1980s are complicated. The reasons for its increasing lack of acceptability in the 1990s will only be speculative at the present time. Let it suffice to say that social work has never been separate from political processes and pressures, either at local or national level. In Britain, direct ministerial intervention with the Central Council of Training in Social Work in 1992 was undoubtedly one of the contributory factors which led to the much diluted and politically more acceptable equal-opportunity policy attached to the new Rules and Requirements for the Diploma in Social Work (CCETSW, 1995). Anti-discriminatory practice was not born in the 1980s or even in the 1970s, although it may have developed a recognisable set of languages that are associated with the debates during those decades. Forsythe (1995) offers an interesting historical contextualisation of anti-discriminatory practice, tracing its origins back to 'the pioneer phase of social work' and linking it to the work of individuals such as Josephine Butler and Elizabeth Fry. Non-discriminatory, anti-discriminatory and anti-oppressive practice, terms that are often used interchangeably but have different meanings and different implications for workers and service users (Thompson, 1993), are not new phenomena. However, the ways in which they have been articulated and their consequences have been specific and different in the recent past. Theoretically, anti-discriminatory practice is now an accepted orthodoxy within the academy and the practice agency, although the variation in this, between different organisations, is still vast.

There is little doubt that social workers and probation officers in almost all settings have been deeply affected by this growth of emphasis on discrimination. A burgeoning literature and an increasing policy emphasis on representation of and sensitive and effective response to members of minority groups reflect the pressures of interest groups and others on policy making and practice. There can be very few social workers today in Britain who are unaware that discrimination and anti-discriminatory practice are major issues at all levels in social work. (Forsythe, 1995)

Anti-discriminatory practice in general may have become an orthodoxy in most areas of social work practice, but anti-discriminatory practice with lesbians and gay men has certainly not. This area has never reached the heady heights of acceptability; equal opportunities policies still sometimes omit the term sexuality or sexual-orientation, or include a tagged-on possible inclusion under such euphemistic phrases as 'other differences' (CCETSW, 1995); there remains a glaring lack of a body of literature specifically about social work with lesbians and gay men, similar to that which has developed in relation to social work and gender or social work and Black communities and, lastly, this area still provokes extreme levels of anxiety, embarrassment and confusion, sometimes resulting in an agency's main priority being that any developments in this area should not attract public attention and real anxiety about drawing the unwanted attention of the media. However, despite the difficulties, considerable progress has been made over the last twenty years within both the field of policy developments and bettering service delivery to lesbians and gay service users and within that of securing better conditions for many lesbians and gay men who deliver those services. To better understand why there has been such a degree of ambivalence in developing a powerful anti-discriminatory discourse in relation to lesbian and gay issues within social work, it is helpful to examine the legislative backdrop that hovers behind and sometimes influences the construction of these conversations.

The legislative backdrop: the British context

CCETSW's equal opportunities policy statement for the Diploma in Social Work reads, 'CCETSW recognises that equal opportunity is something each individual wants for themselves and to which they have a legal right' (1995). Lesbians and gay men in Britain may want this right of equal opportunity but they have no legal right to it. There is no protective legislation that covers the rights of lesbians and gay men such as the Sex Discrimination Act 1975 for women and the Race Relations Act 1976 for Black communities. Clearly it is debatable how much protection or protection of individual rights such legislation gives, but the absence of any legislation can only give none.

There is, however, a substantial body of discriminatory legislation that has negative implications for lesbians and gay men and impacts on social work provision to their communities and to individuals.

The legislation that directly impacts on lesbians and gay men is complex. Reference will only be made to key areas, because this subject has been well documented and comprehensively explored in other key texts (Jeffery-Poulter, 1991; Gooding, 1992; Wilson, 1995). The Criminal Amendment Act 1885 criminalised all forms of sexual activity between men, whether or not these acts were in private or in public. This was also the Act that brought with it the term 'gross indecency'. It was not until the Sexual Offences Act 1967 that male homosexual acts between consenting adults in private were decriminalised. The age of consent for gay men was set at twenty-one, as compared with the heterosexual age of consent which was sixteen. There were many other legal restrictions set around male same-sex activity, including what would be considered private. The definition of private would not hold if there were more than two people involved in the sexual activity or if other persons were present; sex in public lavatories was also outside the definition of private. This first process of decriminalisation of gay male sex applied only to England and Wales. It did not happen in Scotland until 1980 and in Northern Ireland until 1982. There has been no equivalent legislation in relation to lesbian sexual activity, as it has never been legally acknowledged in law, because, as legend has it (and it is only a legend), Queen Victoria believed (we are told) it did not exist. Smith (1995) documents the campaign to lower the age of consent for gay men. This culminated in the inclusion of the lowering of the age from twenty-one to eighteen in the Criminal Justice and Public Order Act 1994. This left the age of consent for male homosexual sexual activity two years older than for hetero-sexual acts. The 1994 Act also introduced the concept of male-on-

male rape onto the statute books and decriminalised homosexuality
in the armed forces and for merchant seamen. However, at the time
of writing, it remains the policy of the Ministry of Defence to
administratively discharge lesbians and gay men from the armed
services. Gay male sexual activity still attracts a disproportionate
amount of the criminal justice system's time and effort, particularly
under the Sexual Offences Act 1956, involving prosecutions for
soliciting and procuring and in relation to definitions of 'private'
under the Sexual Offences Act 1967. For the offence of gross
indecency in 1992 there were 774 prosecutions and 577 convictions
(Palmer, 1995: 50). At the present time, therefore, much gay male
sexual activity is defined as criminal. This clearly has ramifications
for social work practice with gay men, not only in relation to
probation practice.

The 1980s saw the Conservative Party, for many different reasons,
championing a particular and specific model of the nuclear family.
This clashed with increased public awareness and social services
recognition of the diversity of family forms. It also coincided with
the increased confidence and visibility of lesbian mothers. These
different factors coming together in the 1980s contributed to what
can only be described as an obsessive demonisation of lesbian and
gay men on the part of certain sections of the Conservative Party, as
actual or potential, competent carers, a role that had hitherto been
actively denied them (Romans, 1992). At every possible opportunity, the government pursued the same line of argument, trying to
prohibit lesbians and gay men from becoming parents or carers. The
various campaigns and debates surrounding the enactment of Section 28 of the Local Government Act 1988 have been extensively
covered elsewhere (Colvin and Hawksley, 1989, Jeffery-Poulter,
1991; Kaufmann and Lincoln, 1991; Carter, 1992; Wilson, 1995).
This was the Act that introduced the notion of the 'pretend family'.
The Act forbade local authorities to devote resources in such a way
that might be interpreted as 'intentionally promoting' homosexuality and it also prevented schools from 'promoting the teaching in
any maintained school of homosexuality as a pretended family
relationship'. Despite great worries at the time both within social
work (Manning, 1988), and outside it (ROW Policy and Lesbian
Custody Groups, 1988), this piece of legislation has been rarely used
and ironically it may well have had the opposite effect to the one
intended:

legislation aimed at stopping promotion of lesbianism and homo-sexuality unwittingly provoked this very phenomenon. Whenever the law regarding sexuality is changed it signals a redrawing of parameters. The irony is the aim of brushing issues under the carpet with legislation actually causes them to explode into public debates which can paradoxically strengthen the community. (Carter, 1992: 222)

Another commentator notes that the campaigns against section 28 'helped to politicise a new generation of lesbians and gay men (Palmer, 1995: 35). However, it has also been noted that, although this legislation has rarely been used, it may well have influenced reticent local authorities into self-censorship (Smith, 1992; Studzinski, 1994).

The debates surrounding the drafting of the foster placement, guidance and regulations of the Children Act 1989 bore witness to the government using the opportunity to try and limit the capacities of lesbians and gay men to contribute to the wider community as prospective carers. Paragraph 16 of the Department of Health consultation paper reads:

However, authorities and those interested in becoming foster parents must understand that an authority's duty is to find and approve the most suitable foster parents for children who need family placement. It would be wrong arbitrarily to exclude any particular groups of people from consideration. But the chosen way of life of some adults may mean that they would not be able to provide a suitable environment for the care and nurture of a child. No one has a 'right' to be a foster parent. 'Equal rights' and 'gay rights' policies have no place in fostering services. (Department of Health, 1990)

The broad spectrum of childcare agencies involved in the consultation process felt the last sentence was irrelevant and that it was inserted for ideological reasons alone. The final version (Department of Health, 1991c) dropped the reference to 'gay rights' as a result. But the message from the government to, particularly, local authority social services, was loud and clear. The government was not sympathetic to the recruitment and approval of lesbian and gay foster carers.

The next opportunity for the government to prescribe who was and was not fit to parent presented itself in the form of the Human Fertilisation and Embryology Act 1990. The debate relevant to this discussion focused on the rights of lesbians and single women to fertility treatment and specifically to donor insemination (Saffron, 1994). The media treatment of lesbians and gay men and matters relevant to them has been well documented elsewhere (Sanderson, 1995). This particular aspect of the legislation attracted much hostile media attention as well as reasonable discussion and debate (O'Sullivan, 1991; Sage, 1991). Again the government, after consultation, had to back down, and the end result was that the regulatory council covering agencies offering fertilization services had to make sure that they helped users of their services consider the importance of 'the father' for children's development. This inclusion was another example of ideology taking preference over evidence based on research (this will be covered in Chapter 7). Laws relating to adoption were reviewed at the start of the 1990s. This process culminated in the White Paper *Adoption: The Future* (Department of Health, 1993a). This process saw a very similar rerun of the same arguments aired in the consultation process. *The Adoption Law Review Discussion Paper No. 3* included a section on 'lesbians and male homosexuals' which read:

> the question of adoption by lesbians or male homosexuals, whether living with a partner or not, is controversial. There is one view that such applicants should not be excluded from consideration if they can satisfy an agency that they can provide a home in which a child's interests would be safeguarded and promoted. Others take the view that placement with a lesbian or male homosexual could never be in a child's interest and could never provide a suitable environment for the care and nurture of a child. Views would be welcome. (Department of Health, 1991d)

Views poured in, and, despite a quite directive accompanying letter from the then responsible minister which barely concealed his own views, the government again found itself out of line with professional opinion in both social work and childcare fields. The resulting White Paper makes no mention of lesbians and gay men. However it makes very plain that adoption by married couples should be the preferred option other than in 'exceptional circumstances'.

Each time these debates have arisen they have highlighted the degree of homophobia that permeates our society. However, they have also often strengthened the lesbian and gay communities and the working alliances between lesbians and gay men. The resulting legislation has also shown that consultation and lobbying processes still do act as a force to keep in check extreme ideologies that particular governments might favour. However, the end product has often been less than anybody hoped for. Social workers and agencies are left with more professional autonomy than they might have been, but with the distinct impression that lesbian and gay rights or issues are not the flavour of the month.

To summarise, legislation in Britain that has a direct bearing on lesbians and gay men, and on social work practice with them, is organised into two main areas; the sexual practices of gay men, and the capacity of lesbians and gay men to act as parents of and carers for children.

The development of lesbian and gay rights and activism

The ways that homosexuality is described and the discourses surrounding it are radically different from thirty years ago. There are certain aspects associated with it now that did not previously exist, the major ones being visibility, celebration and diversity.

> Homosexuality is not what it used to be. In scarcely a quarter of a century, same-sex experiences in the western world have been ruptured from the simplified, unified, distorting, often medical, frequently criminal, always devalued categories of the past. Instead, they have increasingly become a diverse array of rational, gendered, erotic, political, social, and spiritual experiences. (Plummer, 1992: xiv)

Many commentators on lesbian and gay history would offer different explanations for some of these developments (Weeks, 1991; Plummer, 1992; Cruikshank, 1992; Healey and Mason, 1994; Segal, 1994). There would, however, be a general acceptance of the significance of an event that is often just referred to as 'Stonewall'. In June 1969 when the New York police made one of their regular raids on a gay club, they were met with resistance rather than apology. The resistance spilled out into the street and neighbourhood and the 'rioting' lasted for three days. The Stonewall riots marked a symbolic beginning of resistance, 'gay pride', and the birth of the Gay liberation movement. In Britain, the start of the Gay Liberation Front happened in 1970, in a much less dramatic way. These events led to national and international organisation for lesbian and gay rights. The tangible achievements have been piecemeal and specific to their national contexts. However, there has been a general increase in levels of confidence and visibility in lesbian and gay communities.

What is often referred to as the 'second wave of the women's movement', identified as having its beginning in the 1960s, made an immeasurable difference to lesbian visibility and confidence. Like many historical developments, it is slightly ironic that, at the time, lesbians often experienced feeling marginalised within the movement, while their heterosexual sisters at the same time felt 'dominated by the dykes'. Despite periodic feelings of marginalisation, the feminist movement gave lesbians who were already out, a political and social context which they had often lacked, and enabled many other women, who may not have otherwise had the possibility of coming out, the opportunity of doing so, although a proportion of those were later to 'go back in'. The feminist movement linked lesbianism to feminist political discourses, in such a way as had not been apparent before. Some of the political divisions within feminism were also apparent amongst lesbians, the most relevant to social work being the 'radical feminist' and the 'socialist feminist' divide.

> The differences between Radical and Socialist feminists were to do with priorities. Radical feminists saw men's oppression of women as the fundamental power differential governing society, while Socialist feminists believed that sexual politics was secondary to class politics. (Studzinski, 1994)

Within lesbian and gay activist politics, there has always been and there still remains the polarised binary positions of reformism versus liberation; lobbying versus 'in your face' direct action; reasoned passion versus raw passion. In Britain, these different positions were held in the 1970s by the Campaign for Homosexual Equality (CHE) representing reasoned lobbying, while the Gay Liberation Front (GLF) held the mantle of passionate direct action. Of course, this is just a particular construction of a set of complex realities. Crudely, the 'reformist' position argued for equal rights for lesbians and gay men and access to the same rights as heterosexuals, while the 'transformationists' argued for the deconstruction of notions of gender and sexuality, which would impact on heterosexual individuals and institutions as well as improving the lot of lesbians and gay men. Jeffery-Poulter argues that 'although CHE had initially made a concerted effort to dissociate itself from its more radical rival, as GLF declined it was CHE who benefited directly from the increased awareness and expectations it had awakened' (1991: 109). A similar construction has happened in Britain in the 1990s, Stonewall representing professional political lobbying tactics and Outrage standing for the politics of celebration and transformation. Stonewall was set up in 1989 as a lobbying group with the objective of 'trying to construct a civil rights agenda' (Healey and Mason, 1994: 5). The birth of Outrage, a direct action group, came out of the development of Queer politics, and the post-section 28 campaigns and, to some extent, as part of a backlash to the perceived conformity and prescriptive nature of both the left and feminist politics of the 1980s. It also was a response to the explosion of homophobia which accompanied the discovery of AIDS:

> The AIDS epidemic triggered anger, disbelief and a renewed sense of disenfranchisement among younger lesbians and gay men, who saw the meek acceptance of marginalisation as leading to a dangerous complacency within the community and victimisation from without . . . An urgent sense of mortality inspired the rejection of respectability and discretion. (Smyth, 1992: 11)

The development of Queer politics has been a powerful force, particularly in America, Britain and Australia. A detailed discussion is beyond the remit of this book but is covered in accessible forms elsewhere (Smyth, 1992; Studzinski, 1994). The current perceived split between reformism and transformation politics within the lesbian and gay communities is a powerful construction as all myths are; simple to understand, comforting, with the possibility of identifying with the heroes and heroines and vilifying the baddies. It may be that both are integral, necessary and complementary aspects of a liberation politics, one rarely existing without the other. The component that may well be dysfunctional is the energy that is diverted away from the facilitation of change towards mutual accusation and recrimination.

The developments of lesbian and gay organisation within social work and the arguments for bettering service delivery to the lesbian and gay communities were developed within this context of lesbian and gay activism and could not have happened without it or outside it. The focus and processes that facilitated the thinking about social work and homosexuality would be described as falling within the reasoned, reasonable reformist part of the dichotomy as described above. However, actors in the story of how lesbian and gay issues got onto the social work anti-discriminatory practice agenda often personally occupied both the reformist and the passionate transformationist spaces.

Comparative development: Britain and Australia

Because of the nature of both the oppression of homosexuality internationally and the international nature of many lesbian and gay communities, many developments in one part of the globe are mirrored in another. The effect of individual travellers on this process cannot be underestimated. Jeffery-Poulter, describing some of the repercussions of Stonewall on the British context, gives the following example, of how two individuals who had been in America at a particularly significant moment in lesbian and gay history, became significant players in the development of the Gay Liberation Front in Britain:

> Bob Mellor and Aubrey Walter who had spent their summer vacation in America shared their experience of the new 'gay consciousness' which was transforming the lives of thousands of homosexuals and lesbians on the other side of the Atlantic. Their message fired their audience and within a month meetings were attracting nearly 200 people and a larger venue had to be found. (Jeffery-Poulter, 1991: 99)

There has, over the postwar period, been considerable international lesbian and gay movement, particularly between America, Australia and Britain, and more specifically between San Francisco, Sydney and London. I have chosen to look at the state of New South Wales,

Australia, because its political history over the last twenty years has been somewhat different from that of both Britain and America, who have shared the 'privilege' of right-wing administrations over the majority of that period. When the legislative context for lesbians and gay men was looked at in Britain, there seemed to be a relationship between a right-wing government and attempts to curtail the rights and possibilities for lesbians and gay men. It may, then, be of interest to see how lesbian and gay rights have fared under a slightly more sympathetic administration.

The single major difference between Britain and New South Wales, in relation to law and policy, is that lesbians and gay men in the latter have protective legislation. The Anti-Discrimination Act 1977 set up the Anti-Discrimination Board, which is part of the Attorney General's Department, whose job it was 'to promote anti-discrimination and equal opportunity principles throughout New South Wales' (Anti-Discrimination Board of NSW, 1994a: 4). Discrimination is illegal on the grounds of sex, race, ethnicity, religion, age, marital status, homosexuality and lesbianism and disability within the following contexts: employment, state education, obtaining goods and services, accommodation and registered clubs. Both direct and indirect discrimination are against the law. The Anti-Discrimination Board concentrates its work into three major areas. First, the processing of complaints under the 1977 Act as well as informing people of their rights; second, proactive education programmes and third, reporting to the government regarding necessary changes to the legislation. There are also many more specific functions set out in the legislation.

There have been additional pieces of legislation since 1977 relevant to lesbians and gay men. These are the federal Sex Discrimination Act 1984 and the federal Human Rights and the Equal Opportunity Commission Act 1987. Racial vilification, homosexual vilification and HIV/AIDS vilification are against the law. Homosexual vilification means 'any public act that could encourage hatred, serious contempt or severe ridicule of lesbians and/or gay men' (Anti-Discrimination Board of NSW, 1994b: 1).

As well as, or as a result of, the protective legislation in New South Wales, there is evidence of state department and community co-operation to tackle serious problems facing lesbians and gay men. For example, in 1994 the Streetwatch Implementation Advisory Committee reported its deliberations in relation to how to tackle gay and lesbian bashing in Sydney (Streetwatch Implementation Advisory Committee, 1994). The committee was made up of representatives from a wide range of lesbian and gay community organisations, the Anti-Discrimination Board and seven government departments. Although there have been some important initiatives in Britain in relation to violence against lesbians and gay men (for example, the establishment of lesbian and gay liaison officers by some police forces, Southwark in London being a case in point), Britain is still a long way behind Australia in tackling the problem of violent homophobic attacks.

Stonewall, UNISON and others in Britain have been campaigning to alter the present interpretations of the immigration legislation to allow the recognition of lesbian and gay relationships. At present the Home Office do not do so. 'English law accords no status to homosexual relationships; our immigration practice simply reflects the general position' (UNISON, 1995: 3). Australia has an interdependency model. In 1991, the federal government brought in immigration laws with the new category of 'non-familial relationships of emotional dependency', a category which can cover non-married heterosexual couples as well as lesbian and gay couples. For further discussion see Hart (1992).

Australia is clearly considerably in advance of Britain in both recognising and protecting lesbian and gay rights. Although the impacts on lesbian and gay social work recipients, from these respective countries, has been neither compared nor measured, the very fact that New South Wales has protective legislation and Britain does not would lead us to the conclude that there are likely to be beneficial outcomes from that difference, for New South Wales service users.

It would seem that there might be a link between the comparative progress made in Australia and the political stances of both the federal and State of New South Wales governments. However, in many areas New South Wales has a long way to go, for example, it is similar to Britain in relation to superannuation benefits, which are normally only payable to the spouse or children of the contributor. The age of consent for gay men is eighteen (Crimes Act 1900, New South Wales), the same as in Britain and similarly the age for heterosexual sex is sixteen. According to the Anti-Discrimination Board, there remain on the statute books twenty-nine areas of discrimination against people in gay or lesbian relationships (Anti-

Discrimination Board of NSW, 1994a). Some areas of discrimination place Australian lesbians and gay men in a worse position than their British counterparts, for example in the area of adoption. However, it is argued that lesbians and gay men are in a fundamentally stronger position in New South Wales because of the underlying Anti-Discrimination Law and the role of the Anti-Discriminatory Board, which does not separate lesbians and gay men from other groups, and is there as an arm of the administration to safeguard their interests.

Britain, unlike America, has not developed its struggle for equal rights for lesbian and gay men into a civil rights movement. Britain has no written constitution or current Bill of Rights other than the European Convention on Human Rights, which is not part of British law, making the development of this kind of movement unlikely (Studzinski, 1994). What has been argued for in Britain is both inclusive and exclusive legislative change. By this, I mean legislative change that is exclusive to lesbian and gay men like the Homosexuality Equality Bill put forward by Stonewall, which would include the abolition of the 'inequalities in sexual offences law concerning same-sex behaviour, to outlaw discrimination on the grounds of sexual orientation, and to grant legal recognition to relationships involving lesbians and gay men' (Tatchell, 1992: 238). Inclusive legislation would be similar to the Australian model, of including lesbians and gay men into a more general piece of legislation that would cover all areas of discrimination. Tatchell argues that this would place 'legislative initiatives for homosexual equality within a broader agenda of "equal rights for all"' (1992: 240). How he proposes to actualise this is very similar to the New South Wales model: 'full equality in law, legal protection against discrimination, equality of access and opportunity and positive action to monitor, promote, and enforce equality' (1992: 240). These principles, according to Tatchell, would be achieved for everyone through a Bill of Rights, an Anti-Discrimination Act and a Department for Equal Opportunities. The similarities with the Australian model are striking. Although lesbian and gay rights in that country still have a long way to go before we can talk of real equality, tremendous gains have been achieved. It may also mean that different groups have the possibility of working together rather than being pitched against each other in a metaphorical competition for equal rights. Importantly, it may also give both lesbian and gay communities and individuals a degree of confidence, a springboard, for further reforms and changes.

Britain in the 1980s: a case study of the potentialities arising out of contradictions

This chapter has argued that there may be a relationship between Britain having had a right-wing administration since 1979 and the concerted efforts that have been made during the same period to limit the rights of lesbians and gay men. However, the same period has witnessed some improvements; for example, the lowering of the age of consent for gay men. There can be little argument that the position of lesbians and gay men, despite the government's intentions, has changed fundamentally, not necessarily through legislative changes but through gradual policy and cultural shifts. It is worth reproducing in full what Studzinski refers to as 'some of the positive signs':

> in 1990 the first lesbian and gay television series, *Out On Tuesday*, was broadcast on Channel 4. . .
>
> in 1992 the first STD (sexually transmitted diseases) clinic specifically for lesbians, the Bernhard clinic, was opened at Charing Cross Hospital in London. . .
>
> in May 1993 Amnesty International adopted its first gay prisoners of conscience. . .
>
> in October 1993 two Scottish lesbians sacked for their sexual orientation won an out-of-court settlement in a case alleging sex discrimination. . .
>
> in November the BBC issued guidelines banning the stereotyping of lesbians and gays. . .
>
> in 1993 and 1994 innovative lesbian characters appeared in Channel 4's *Brookside*, the comedy series *Roseanne* and BBC programmes *Rides* and *EastEnders*. . .
>
> in May 1994 the Lord Chancellor announced that sexual orientation will no longer be taken into account when appointing judges. . .
>
> in June 1994 a lesbian co-parent was awarded joint custody of a child with the biological mother. . .

by mid-1994 there were eight glossy lesbian and/or gay magazines available nationally.

(Studzinski, 1994: 55)

Healey and Mason also note:

> it would be difficult not to sense a feeling of optimism and hope about lesbian and gay politics. At the 'fag' end of the twentieth century, as other progressive movements fail and falter, lesbian and gay men are the one social group for whom life seems to be getting better. (Healey and Mason, 1994: 3)

My suspicion would be that this degree of optimism may be the case for many lesbians and gay men, but for others the day-to-day realities of life may well not have been radically affected by some of the changes and political shifts outlined in this chapter. For many lesbian and gay clients/service users, as for the majority of clients and service users, the major preoccupation may well be poverty, the great equaliser, where there is little room for optimism. However, some of the developments, outlined above, that have led to the strengthening of lesbian and gay men's position in Britain, are likely to have benefited lesbian and gay social workers, and have impacted on the creation of policies that have both directly and indirectly improved the thinking within some social work agencies, about the quality of service provision to lesbians and gay men.

The preoccupations of lesbians and gay activists, academics, writers, performers, media workers and commentators may be very different from the silent majority of lesbians and gay men. One area where there was a conscious attempt to bring these two often separate forces together was in attempts to improve the lot of the lesbian and gay communities through local government initiatives during the 1980s (Cooper, 1994). The development of thinking about anti-discriminatory social work practice is firmly located within this period and was geographically located within the Labour-controlled boroughs and metropolitan areas. This is not to say that there had not been other developments at other times in other places, but that this was the period and these the locations where others' work came to fruition.

I have argued elsewhere that 'three separate movements have affected local authorities' policies in relation to lesbians and gay men' (Brown, 1992a: 206), these being changes within the Labour Party, the lead being given by the Greater London Council (GLC) to other local authorities, and developments within the trade union movement. Although I still think this, like all historical observations this one is flawed by being too dependent on what is documented through the written word. An immensely important omission has been the unrecorded struggles of individual social workers and service users/clients to improve practice and service provision. Another would be the grassroots lesbian and gay community involvement with local government developments (Cooper, 1994).

To fully understand how and why matters that were relevant to lesbians and gay men found themselves on the social work agenda in the 1980s would be complex and beyond the scope of this chapter. What can be said is that it was partly to do with the complex interrelationships between the different systems outlined above. Several of the actors involved in specific systems would have occupied more than one stage at any one time.

An example of the complex interrelationships during that period would be the processes involved between the Labour Party and the trade unions, specifically the National Association of Local Government Officers (NALGO – now absorbed in UNISON) in negotiating changes in local authorities' policies. 'The 1980s saw a growing commitment to lesbian and gay rights within the trade unions – again, largely as a result of the New Left politics developed within Labour councils' (Studzinski, 1994: 36). Of course, many involved with the NALGO lesbian and gay group during that time would argue that the process was exactly the opposite. The truth may be that so many individual activists were involved in both arenas, that it is pointless to attempt to ascertain which was the chicken and which the egg. The most comprehensive analysis of these issues in this period is offered by Cooper:

> the emergence of lesbian and gay issues on the agenda of local government was a process which witnessed a change in both the Labour Party and the lesbian and gay movements. The former shifted towards formal support for equal rights, while the latter moved in the direction of demands for affirmation and anti-discriminatory initiatives, away from a politics which privileged sexuality or gender as the originary motor for 'fundamental' social change. (Cooper, 1994: 37)

The relevant developments within the Labour Party have been documented elsewhere (Tobin, 1990; Roelofs, 1991; Brown, 1992a; Cooper, 1994; Studzinski, 1994). A key development was the setting up of the Labour Campaign for Gay Rights (LCGR), a broad-based organisation involving the Labour Party and trade unions. These sorts of developments were not happening in isolation, but alongside the hard-fought-for and gradual acceptance of the autonomous organisation of oppressed groups within both the Labour Party and trade unions. 1981 saw the change of the organisation's name to the Labour Campaign for Lesbian and Gay Rights (LCLGR). In 1985 both the Labour Party and the Trade Union Congress passed resolutions supporting lesbian and gay rights (Labour Campaign for Lesbian and Gay Rights, 1986). The Labour Party's resolution was updated in 1988 to include the Party's commitment to repeal section 28. The Labour Party 1992 election manifesto included the following:

> We will introduce a new law dealing with discrimination on grounds of sexuality, repeal the unjust Clause 28 and allow a free vote in the House of Commons on the age of consent. (Labour Party, 1992)

A central focus for these developments was the Greater London Council (GLC), under the leadership of Ken Livingstone. The Conservative Party were able to focus a lot of their concerns over the autonomy of local authorities onto the GLC and often used lesbian and gay issues to fuel hostility towards 'the loony left'. The Press was highly influential at this time, the GLC and particularly Ken Livingstone being demonised as wasters of ratepayers' money by focusing on such groups as lesbians and gay men (Sanderson, 1995). The GLC was fundamentally important in trying to realise some policy changes affecting lesbians and gay men and inevitably some of these attempts were flawed (Tobin, 1990), but they had a profound impact on thinking in relation to service delivery within many local authorities. This period saw the development of the lesbian and gay units within some local authorities. For a more detailed history and analysis, see Cooper (1994). The GLC undoubtedly had an impact on this process.

The GLC was also influential in establishing a belief that local authorities should try to liaise with the communities they represented. Liaising with lesbian and gay communities and trying to involve them in processes of consultation is a complex affair. Who represents and speaks for those communities? How do you consult with individuals you cannot identify because they are not out? Are those lesbians and gay men who are active and vociferous within their communities likely to be representative of those who are not? Whatever the high expectations and the inevitable disappointments of the time, the GLC was radical. The Conservative Party appreciated this, even if some activists did not. The government's response was decisive: the GLC had to be abolished – and it was, in March 1986. In its death throes, it left an important legacy for social work in the form of two publications (GLC and the GLC Gay Working Party, 1985; GLC, 1986). Cooper has argued that 'discrimination in housing and social services provision was experienced by lesbians and gays, in the main, on an individualistic basis' (Cooper, 1994). The GLC publications helped in a small way to change this by examining social service provision, along with other local authority provision, and by making some well-argued facilitative suggestions about the improvement of service delivery to lesbians and gay men.

The autonomous organisation of lesbians and gay men within NALGO (the trade union that had the most direct impact on social work) mirrored many of the developments within the Labour Party, although many predated them. An examination of the influences of the relevant trade unions will follow (Chapter 4). The development of equal opportunities policies within local authorities was a complex negotiation between relevant groups, NALGO often being a main player. From the mid-1970s, lesbians and gay men within NALGO were actively involved in trying to secure lesbian and gay rights. The first national lesbian and gay conference ever in Britain was organised by lesbian and gay NALGO activists and was held in October 1984. Much NALGO activity centred around supporting lesbians and gay men who because of their sexual-orientation had been sacked or otherwise discriminated against. NALGO was centrally involved in trying to get sexuality included into local authority equal opportunities policies. The major significance for social work of all this was that, while campaigning for workers' conditions of service, NALGO never separated off the rights of service users, and was therefore influential in helping place lesbians and gay men on the anti-discriminatory practice agenda.

Changes within the Labour Party, the influence of the GLC experience and the close relationship between some local authorities and NALGO, which was becoming more receptive to the demands of its lesbian and gay lobby, meant that, as a first step, many local authorities did include sexual orientation into their equal opportunities policies during the 1980s. Given the political and legislative backdrop of that period, this was a major achievement. Those policies offered the workforce some protection that legislation denied them. That, I believe, was fundamentally important in enabling social workers to begin to look at service provision and their practice with lesbians and gay men. These small achievements enabled lesbians and gay men within social work to be more vocal. Developments within some local authorities eventually had an impact on CCETSW, who in turn added sexual orientation to its policies for both employees and (more importantly for social work) in its capacity as a validating body, which subsequently impacted on social work education.

The next agenda

Lesbians and gay men in Britain have been the subjects of a major contradictory process; a central government intent on the vilification of homosexuality and limiting rights and, at the same time, some local governments pursuing the realisation of lesbian and gay rights. The impact on social workers of this dynamic will be discussed later (Chapter 4). Lesbian and gay cultures are now noteworthy because of the degree of their diversity. It would be impossible and inaccurate to talk about a lesbian and gay community, or about lesbian and gay issues, as if they were obviously identifiable and uniform. The struggles for lesbian and gay rights since Stonewall have had a profound impact on many areas relevant to social work, particularly on local authorities, still the major social work employer. The last thirty years and particularly the last ten have been a period of change and turmoil. The next agenda needs to include some of the detail of how we, really do, deliver a competent, anti-oppressive social work service to lesbians and gay men.

4

Lesbians and Gay Men in Social Work

We can safely assume that there have always been lesbians and gay men involved in social work, both as service providers and as service users. One of the problems of quantifying the numbers involved, even if it were relevant or useful, would be that the majority of people would have remained in the closet whether they were clients/service users or providers. Social work has had tremendous difficulties in accepting homosexuality as a valid sexual choice equal to heterosexuality (Hart and Richardson, 1981; Kus, 1990a; Brown, 1992a). Traditionally, social work has either ignored the issue or over-focused on it. Writing specifically about lesbians, Brown says:

> in practice, social work agencies tend to deal with lesbians in one of two ways. Either the woman's specific needs as a lesbian remain unrecognised and ignored, or her lesbianism becomes the central preoccupation, the prism through which her every word and action is interpreted. (Brown, 1992a: 201)

In addition to ordinary run-of-the-mill homophobia, which is likely to be as prevalent in social work as in any other professional work force (Tievsky, 1988), much of social work's difficulties with this area lie with its theoretical underpinning and its choice of a relevant theoretical base which it sought out and chose as part of its process of professionalisation (see Chapter 5).

Discrimination

We do not know a lot about what service users think about the service they receive, despite, within the British context, there being an obligation to seek their views in some areas of provision (Department of Health, 1989). When we do hear what clients and service users have to say it is often quite a shock. The publication *The Client Speaks*, which consisted of working-class impressions of casework, published in 1970 (Mayer and Timms), offered a detailed documentation of the views of casework recipients, and remains one of the most important publications within social work. Daniel, writing the foreword to that publication, noted one of the reasons why the Family Welfare Association had agreed to take part in the study: 'it was thought that client opinion would be immediately relevant to the staff of FWA and probably to other social workers and teachers of social work as well' (Mayer and Timms, 1970: vii). She was right. To hear the client's perspective of a service is clearly of help to both clients and providers. We know even less about lesbian and gay service users' experience of social work than we do of the general clientele.

However, slightly more is known about the experience of the lesbian and gay workers who provide these services and interventions. Given that homosexual service users and providers are at the receiving end of the same form of oppression, although it would be wrong to equate their different realities, it might be assumed that their experiences of discrimination or anti-discrimination within social work may have some similarities, although their differential access to power is likely to affect those experiences. Another key consideration must be that, for all sorts of complex reasons, different individuals experience the same discriminatory acts and oppression differently. We should never assume a uniform response to oppression, or uniform perceptions of it. The fate of lesbian and gay service users at the receiving end of social work may well reflect the experiences of the lesbian and gay service providers within social work.

There is still considerable fear and anxiety among lesbian and gay social workers about their agencies' responses to lesbians and gay men generally and towards lesbian and gay social work employees specifically. For historical reasons, as indicated in the previous chapter, tremendous improvements have taken place within many social work settings in relation to the levels of security offered to the lesbian and gay workforce. History is important, in that it helps us locate ourselves in the present by contextualising the processes that enabled us to arrive there. Historical events can take on symbolic meaning far beyond the significance of the specific happening. Three such events that have affected lesbian and gay social workers, both directly and indirectly, are the sacking of Susan Shell in 1981, the sacking of Judith Williams in 1982 and the struggle involving Rugby Council in 1984, and Stockport in 1985. Although these events happened a considerable time ago, the legacy of anxiety they left behind has reverberated for years, even though those affected by this anxiety may not be aware of the originating events. Both the events of 1981 and 1982 became a focus for NALGO activity and became part of a strengthening argument for lesbian and gay employment rights, particularly within social work, where the position of lesbians and gay men was perceived as being very vulnerable. The reasons for this vulnerability were partly to do with two powerful myths: the belief that lesbians and, more particularly, gay men are more likely to abuse children and that homosexuality can be somehow 'promoted' and therefore potential lesbian and gay 'role models' should be kept away from children and young people.

Susan Shell and Judith Williams were both working with young people. When Susan Shell's sexual orientation became known to her employers (because she told them) at the hostel for adolescent girls where she was employed, she was suspended. There followed a tribunal, made up of council members, where the decision was upheld, seemingly purely on the grounds of her unsuitability because of her lesbianism. Davis records the social work press reporting that the local authority's responses to the union's questions included the following: 'it is the responsibility of social services departments to encourage the socio-sexual norms of marriage and children in the young people in their care, and it was not prepared to debate the philosophy of homosexuality' (1993: 60). Judith Williams was dismissed from her post as a residential social worker within a voluntary establishment for adolescent girls. The employers in this case described her as 'temperamentally unsuitable', while its 'general policy on the staff' stated that 'such persons should be mature, stable adults who identify with the conventional adult model normally accepted by society' (Davis, 1993: 61).

Given that there is no protective legislation in Britain for lesbians and gay men, the inclusion of sexual orientation into employers' equal opportunities and employment policies has been profoundly important for lesbian and gay employees and job applicants. This has been particularly important within local authorities and has had special significance within social work, a profession that was often reluctant to employ out lesbians and gay men in the past. When Rugby Council, under a Conservative leadership, decided in 1985 to delete sexual orientation from its policy relating to employment, a powerful campaign in opposition was mounted, which was successful in that a more sympathetic policy was subsequently developed. However, it made many feel uneasy that hard-fought-for policies could so easily be swept away, leaving lesbian and gay workers with no protection against discrimination. This event also released a torrent of media homophobia. Although the media do not create homophobia, they certainly fuel it. Sanderson records the *Sun*'s response to Rugby on 28 September 1984:

> Hooray for Rugby! The Tory council has scrapped a guarantee that it will not discriminate against homosexuals seeking jobs. Farmer Gordon Collett declares robustly: 'We're not having men turning up for work in dresses and earrings.' Dead right! The Sun has nothing against homosexuals. What they do in private is their own affair. But they have no right to make their closet problems our problems. For years we have had to endure a campaign to cast homosexuals first as martyrs and then as heroes. Some employers have even been bullied into giving them preference for jobs . . . The homosexuals have been led to believe that they are superior, healthy and normal while the rest of the community are out of step. A society which swallows that kind of sick nonsense is in danger of destroying itself. Let's ALL follow Rugby in fighting back! (Sanderson, 1995: 154)

Although the rantings of a *Sun* journalist can be dismissed as an irrelevance, it does not feel like that for individuals against whom those generalised rantings are directed. In 1985, Stockport refused to include lesbians and gay men in their equal opportunities policy for employment. After another national campaign and demonstration, they eventually, in 1986, changed the policy to include sexual orientation.

These examples of local authorities' hostility to lesbians and gay men offer two contradictory messages for lesbians and gay men in social work. First, they can never be complacent: despite the inclusion of sexual orientation in equal opportunities policies, so long as no legislation exists in this area, a change in the ideology of the local administration may cause such policies to be overturned. Second, both examples gave rise to some degree of optimism, because they showed the power of organised collective action – both Rugby and Stockport retracted.

As employees, lesbian and gay social workers are, thus, vulnerable to political whim. It may be politically expedient to support their desire for employment security and freedom from discrimination one year but not the next. While lesbians and gay men are left outside anti-discrimination legal frameworks, this very real insecurity will remain. The best that can be obtained at present are robust equal opportunities and anti-discriminatory policies that secure the position of service providers and users alike. Clients/service users cannot be expected to approach a social work agency with any degree of confidence if the workforce itself doesn't have any protection against discrimination. We cannot expect social workers to engage in complex practice issues with lesbians and gay men when they feel that they are, literally, working at the level of arguing for those clients to have a legitimate right to their sexuality as a valid, equal sexuality, and that their clients/service users' sexual orientation is the only aspect of those individuals' complex realities that ever gets focused upon. Anti-discriminatory policies are the first step in insisting that lesbians and gay men, both as providers and users of services, have a right to the same quality of employment conditions and services as all other people; that they must be viewed as whole, complex, unique individuals like anyone else, and, also like anyone else, sometimes things go wrong and they may need social work services or interventions.

Coming out

One of the serious repercussions of oppression for lesbians and gay men is that some choose to hide their sexuality, as a result of discrimination or the belief that they will be discriminated against. The psychological impacts of homophobia are various and will depend on the specificity of the individual concerned. One response to oppression, in the form of homophobia, is the process of the possible internalisation or identification with the oppressive beliefs or behaviours. Individuals may, consciously or unconsciously, believe themselves to be inferior or sick or a genetic oddity or deserving of abuse – i.e. to be sympathised with, even to be protected and tolerated, but never to be different and equal, because that would threaten the hegemony of heterosexuality's superiority. Certain groups are not only oppressed from outside but often oppress themselves from inside, both from within their own communities and within their own heads and psyches.

Some of the social work literature on working with lesbians and gay men has arisen out of humanistic approaches in America and is very much from what I will describe as the 'Gays-can-be-happy-too' school of thought. This material is developed by lesbian and gay social workers, counsellors and therapists. It tends to arise from the idea that there is a gay gene, the consequent argument being, 'If these people can't help it then societies should be nice to them and protect them'. This argument was prevalent during 1995 because of the research work of Hamer in America. Despite the evidence being scientifically thin and methodologically limited, it stimulated popular interest. The results have been in relation to gay men: the same findings have never been 'proven' for women. However, there has often been a strong desire among some lesbians and gay men to believe that homosexuality is genetically defined, and therefore they can't help their sexual desires for members of their own sex. This 'victim of genetic make-up' position has political ramifications quite different from the idea that all forms of sexuality are social constructions. To 'choose' to be homosexual is deviant, and a different set of social and political consequences follow. The genetics-versus-social construction arguments are beyond the remit of this book except to say that the 'Gays-can-be-happy-too' lobby has been powerful within American social work discourses and has sometimes reinforced stereotypes. Kus's work, which includes some important and invaluable contributions (Kus, 1990b), has a chapter on coming out that includes the following in his discussion of lesbian and gay development:

> Very little is known about gay and lesbian children, and virtually nothing is known about gay and lesbian infants. Biological advances will, undoubtedly, go far in helping us understand more as we learn how gays are different biologically from other males, and how lesbians are different from other females. Researchers such as Gladue, Green, and Hellman, who have found biochemical responses differing between gay and straight men, may

eventually conduct studies to learn the differences in childhood and infancy. (Kus, 1990b: 31)

He continues:

> Like the gay boy, the lesbian girl is also a maverick. She too realises that she is somehow 'different' from other girls. But unlike the gay boy, she often exhibits the 'Rubyfruit-Jungle Syndrome'. . . This syndrome is characterised by assertiveness, a desire to compete equally with boys, bucking traditionally 'feminine' trappings of dress and behaviour, and keen interest in sports and traditional heterosexual male activities.

Although this can be viewed as a quaint stereotype where the author seems to be oblivious of any of the feminist discourses of the last thirty years which address the construction of 'femininity' and how that might impact on all women, heterosexual or lesbian, it is, nevertheless, a highly influential book, precisely because of the paucity of writing in this area which is of any relevance to social work. Many readers would be unlikely to contextualise such arguments in order to make better sense of them. This type of writing, reinforcing particular stereotypes and 'common-sense' assumptions based on little more than opinion (which lacks any sound research base), is as prevalent among lesbian and gay authors as it is among heterosexuals. The problem with this is that, for all sorts of complex political reasons that arose out of what is referred to as the 'politics of identity' (which was at its height in the 1980s), it became an accepted orthodoxy that: first, only members of a particular oppressed group could talk about that particular oppression; second, if a member of a particular group spoke about that oppression, what they said was 'fact' or 'truth', not just their perception from the specificity of their particular experience; and third, for others to challenge those perceptions that established themselves as truths was, by definition, oppressive. The development of this orthodoxy lay in the history of oppressed groups always having been spoken for, or talked about. However, nothing is so guaranteed to silence dialogue, and without dialogue there is no possibility of change. This might mean that stereotyping material written by lesbians and gay men might have more influence than material written by heterosexual writers that could be simply dismissed as homophobic.

This then leads to an effective internal policing process among lesbians and gay men – a form of identification with oppression.

These beliefs around the causation of homosexuality are important because they affect lesbians' and gay men's sense of themselves and the processes of coming out. Coming out can have two separate but related meanings: first, the term is often associated with a person's first same-sex sexual experience, meaning that the individual has a realisation at any point in their life that they are sexually attracted to a member or members of their own sex; second, the conscious realisation of this, being followed by 'telling' others, to make this knowledge known to friends, colleagues and relatives, and to be identified with, or identifying with 'the lesbian and gay community'. This process of coming out, particularly in relation to the second meaning, is associated with a high level of stress. For many people, the process of telling their families is particularly stressful and many people never do. Some people are out in certain situations and not others. One of the most difficult aspects of coming out is that it is a never-ending process, each new situation requires another telling. In the main, as sexual-orientation isn't visually obvious and the assumption is often made that people are all heterosexual, this is a fairly constant and exhausting process. Large numbers of people never come out at work, and this does seem to be particularly difficult in social work:

> Fear of losing our jobs is not the only reason lesbian and gay social workers hide our sexuality. This all too realistic fear is aggravated by institutionalised and internalised oppression. In addition there are some aspects of our professionalism such as concepts of 'neutrality' and 'professional distance' which act as further barriers to our coming out. (Hillin, 1985)

Lesbian and gay social workers are aware of the profession's historical difficulty with accepting homosexuality as anything other than pathology (see Chapter 5). If workers find being and coming out difficult, then social work clients/service users are also likely to find this problematic.

Both clients/service users and workers may decide that the actual or potential cost of coming out is too high. Individuals' decisions about this will be dictated by their own particular situation. There may, though, be additional considerations for groups of lesbians

and gay men who experience the interrelationships of more than one
form of oppression, Black lesbians and gay men being a case in
point. White lesbians and gay men are no more renowned for their
anti-racist struggles than any other group of white people, and Black
lesbians and gay men may not experience much solidarity and
support from their homosexual brothers and sisters. Lesbian and
gay culture, writing, politics and organisation have been dominated
by white people. Black lesbians and gay men have sometimes felt
marginalised, talked for and about, but rarely with, stereotyped and
over-eroticised. This state of play is changing, but only slowly. These
factors mean that some Black lesbians and gay men, who feel they
cannot rely on the lesbian and gay community for support, may
decide that dealing with racism and homophobia simultaneously is,
understandably, too much, and decide to focus on managing the
racism and not coming out in certain settings. However, it is
important to note that large numbers of Black lesbians and gay
men have consistently fought oppression on both fronts, and the
inclusion of the rights of lesbians and gay men in the new 1995
South African constitution is a testament to their bravery and
commitment to tackle oppression in whatever form.

It is not just in South Africa that such developments have taken
place. In 1990, the Black lesbian and gay community formed Black
Lesbians and Gays Against Media Homophobia (BLAGAMH).
This group, with the support of NALGO, initiated a successful
campaign against *The Voice*, a Black newspaper which had been
publishing homophobic material. This campaign acted as a politicis-
ing process for many social workers, as it was brought to their
attention because of a NALGO ban on placing advertisements in
The Voice. This campaign was another success. For many Black
lesbians and gay men their own Black families and communities are
a very real source of support and refuge against racism. Mason-John
and Khambatta, writing about the process of coming out for Black
lesbians, argue that, although there can be more openness about
sexuality:

> to come out as a lesbian in a Black community can still be
> traumatic. And some communities still disown their lesbian
> daughters. Many Black women see their communities as a safe
> space in which they are protected from the institutionalised and
> individual racism they experience in Britain. So for many Black

lesbians, the support of their communities is of great importance. (Mason-John and Khambatta, 1993: 24)

There has been a real expansion in the field of literature relevant to the experiences of Black lesbians and gay men, which will help the social work profession as well as, hopefully, supporting the experiences of individual Black lesbians and gay men (Nevins, 1991; Mason-John and Khambatta, 1993; Cole Wilson and Allen, 1994; Ejo, 1994; Mason-John, 1995).

We can never make the assumption that lesbians and gay men will be out or should be out. That will be an individual decision, depending on the life circumstances of that person. However, the costs to individuals of having to hide their sexuality, to sometimes lie about or evade discussion arising about their lifestyles, has serious consequences. The more lesbians and gay men are able to be out, the stronger the position of all lesbians and gay men. For those that have some access to power, it is important to consider the impact created on others who have less access to power, by their own personal decision about being out or not. An example would be a social services team leader who is a lesbian and remains in the closet. She may convey an atmosphere of fear to lesbian and gay men and to service users. If the providers of a service are unable to come out, they will work with lesbian and gay men in limited ways. If clients and service users cannot come out to the social work personnel because of real or perceived homophobia, this will profoundly affect the quality of any provision or intervention they may receive, as it will be premised on false information.

The only way of safeguarding the quality of services received by the lesbian and gay communities is to provide a social work context within which diversity is welcomed, rather than rejected.

Social work education: production of the professional

Lessons on the dangers of being out in social work happen in the seminar rooms for students on social work training courses. Logan *et al.*'s book, which addresses lesbian and gay issues in social work education, is the first one of its kind in Britain, both to describe this process and to look at ways of tackling it (Logan *et al.*, 1996). Historically, social work training was hostile to the recruitment of lesbians and gay men, using arguments similar to those still used by some British psychoanalytic training organisations. Ellis, who surveyed the attitudes of various psychoanalytical and psychotherapeutic British training institutions on accepting lesbian and gay men for training, concluded:

> The dearth of critical questioning by psychoanalysts of their own theoretical position has serious implications for lesbians and gay candidates for training. Specifically, the unquestioned centrality of the Oedipus complex in the specification of gender and sexual identity, by definition excludes such candidates from psycho-analytic and psychoanalytic psychotherapy training. (Ellis, 1994)

Social work and social work education has been greatly influenced by psychoanalytic orthodoxy (Yelloly, 1980; Pearson *et al.*, 1988). The close relationship between the two has left a legacy within social work training of viewing homosexuality as pathology.

> The majority of social work courses teach that homosexuality is a pathology, a form of social deviance that is to be studied but not condoned. They teach that the nuclear family is the ideal, and children may be at risk if reared in other circumstances. (GLC and GLC Gay Working Party, 1985: 28)

My own view is that this was a slightly exaggerated perception which, certainly by 1985, was not the case on all social work courses. Homophobia is transmitted in much subtler forms on social work courses today. By this, I am not suggesting there is no possibility that some courses might still convey explicit homophobic views, but such courses are likely to be in the minority, partly due to CCETSW's explicit inclusion of non-discrimination towards lesbians and gay men in their equal opportunities policy when validating social work programmes.

I organise under four headings the ways in which social work education acts in oppressive ways towards lesbians and gay men, which, in turn, influence whether they feel comfortable about coming out. First come the homophobic attitudes expressed by fellow students that are sometimes not engaged with by tutors; which are either silenced, as being politically incorrect or ignored. Social work students are likely to be no more or less homophobic than the rest of the population and social work educators need to be able to engage students in exploration of their attitudes. This may mean managing conflictual discussion, but is the only way of facilitating the exploration of attitudes and the possibility of facilitating change. Social work educators who do engage in such work also hold the responsibility of making sure that individual lesbians and gay men are in no way abused through those discussions. If negative views about homosexuality are silenced or ignored in social work courses, thus not allowing any exploration or potential for change, then those attitudes are much more likely, later on, to be translated into negative behaviours towards lesbian and gay service users.

Second, social work knowledge is problematic in many ways (to be explored in Chapter 5). Unless aspects of that knowledge are contextualised, or the methodology of its research base is questioned, it can be perceived as homophobic. The teaching of developmental psychology, for example, often relies heavily on texts that just refer to heterosexual experience. Much of such material is also directly relevant to lesbians and gay men, but unless there is an explicit reference made to the specific nature of such material or the need to rethink some of it, to critically analyse it and address the question of its relevance to all people or just specific groups, it is likely to be rejected as homophobic, or accepted as universally applicable to all people, without modification.

Third, in order for social workers to be adequately equipped to meet the needs of their lesbian and gay clients, they need to be made aware of relevant research and knowledge that might be specific to lesbian and gay lives. The omission of such a knowledge base from courses can be experienced as homophobic by lesbian and gay students.

Last, whether or not lesbians and gay students feel safe enough to come out on courses will be dependent on their perception of the level of support they might receive from tutors if they were, as a result of being open about their sexuality, to be at the receiving end of discrimination, either on their fieldwork placements or in the college setting.

As indicated earlier in this chapter, there is likely to be a relationship between the level of security felt by lesbians and gay men in social work in their places of work (which either enables or inhibits them from being out) and the corresponding experiences of lesbian

Social Work and Sexuality

and gay clients and the quality and appropriateness of the services they receive. The same relationship is relevant to the processes of social work education. Unless there is an atmosphere of respecting and valuing difference, cultivated within educational and training establishments, then the four considerations outlined above are less likely to be realised. This culture of the valuing of diversity needs to be backed by equal opportunities policies conveying the message that discrimination against lesbians and gay men is unacceptable and that lesbians and gay men will be able to work in those places, and be open about their sexual orientation, free from harassment and discrimination.

Those policies must be developed within each educational establishment and training agency. In countries that are not directed by legislation to do so, whether or not to include, support and enforce equal opportunities policies relating to sexual orientation remains the individual decision of each establishment. In Britain, those lesbians and gay men who work in the university sector, if they are union members, are covered by policies developed by UNISON, the Association of University Teachers (AUT) and the University and College Lecturers' Union (NATFHE). UNISON's policies, are by far the most sophisticated and highly developed, as a result of lesbian and gay activity over many years within NALGO (now part of UNISON; see Chapter 6). The AUT developed a paper in 1991 which covered sexual orientation and employment in universities. The AUT had incorporated sexual orientation into their equal opportunities policy by 1987, some ten years later than NALGO. The AUT 1991 document, as well as covering employment and service and conditions issues, also comments on curriculum: 'In teaching, no uncritical or insensitive use should be made which deals with issues involving sexual orientation' (AUT, 1991: 2). In 1988 the AUT made a very powerful statement in response to section 28 (see Chapter 3). It is worth reproducing a section of this, as it shows the degree of anxiety generated by the passing of the legislation and the possible impact it could have on education:

> Council deplores and repudiates 'Clause 28' of the Local Government Bill and affirms its belief in the fundamental rights of lesbians and gay men of equality before the law, in the work place and within education. Council is specifically concerned (a)

that the clause will disrupt the free and open exchange of ideas within universities, polytechnics and colleges; (b) that the existence of lesbian and gay student societies will be threatened; (c) that lecturers must be allowed freedom of expression concerning the questions of sexual morality that their subjects may raise; and (d) that the conscience of university tutors who have to advise students on personal matters should not be fettered. Council welcomes the contribution made by lesbian and gay members of universities and defends their right to work and study without harassment or censorship. (AUT, 1991: 3)

NATFHE have developed a considerable amount of material relating to the employment rights of lesbians and gay men, since the inclusion of sexual orientation into its equal opportunities policy by 1984, although it had passed important supportive motions at conference in 1982 (NATFHE, 1986). These include harassment at work guidelines (NATFHE, 1994a), a guide to language (NATFHE, 1993), and a practice guide for equal opportunities policies for negotiators (NATFHE, 1994b). NATFHE have also made the link between the political and legal position of lesbians and gay men and the curriculum:

public attitudes have been shaped by discriminatory legislation against lesbians and gay men, and [Council] is aware that particular efforts will be necessary to explain and promote a lesbian and gay equality policy. The false impression that it is not possible under the law to raise issues around sexuality and to present an accurate image of lesbians and gay men in the classroom needs to be challenged. (NATFHE, 1994b: 12)

Social work educators are backed by policies from both the relevant unions about teaching appropriate curriculums covering lesbian and gay material, as well as lesbians and gay men as lecturers having their employment rights safeguarded. However, it is up to the individual college or university to also develop their own policies. For students to be able to learn and for lecturers to be able to teach effectively, both groups need to feel safe and comfortable. Lesbians and gay men will feel neither safe nor comfortable if they cannot be out in their place of learning or teaching.

Last word

The key objective for social work agencies must be to deliver a good-enough service to the public. It is commonly accepted that about 10 per cent of the public is homosexual. However, that acceptance has little basis in fact. When the methodological approaches and methods of some of the research in this area are scrutinised, the 10 per cent can only ever be seen as an estimate:

> Even with the most advanced techniques of quantitative research, prevalence estimates are little more than cultural artefacts. The meaning of the measurement changes. The scaling down of sexuality to numerical values creates the impression that the score reflects some fixed and underlying trait, but this is more illusory than real. whatever is being measured is not a permanent position determined by nature, but a fluid and dynamic characteristic, contingent upon social context. (Creith, 1996: 83)

Social work agencies have the same responsibilities to members of this lesbian and gay population (whatever its number) that contact them as they do to heterosexual service users. Part of the attempt to deliver a good enough service will involve the creation of cultures within agencies that do not discriminate against lesbians and gay men, either in employment or service delivery, and which respect and value diversity. Social work education also has to engage in the same process. A qualifying social worker needs to be adequately equipped by their acquisition of relevant knowledge, values and skills to offer a competent service. This will require them, as a crucial aspect of the learning process, to seek out applicable knowledge relevant to each new situation or service user and to critically evaluate that knowledge by locating it within its own context and evaluating its relevance accordingly.

5

Social Work Knowledge – Revisited

Social work knowledge is problematic for many reasons. One reason is that social workers' use of aspects of such knowledge may have contributed to the discrimination against lesbians and gay men with whom they came into contact. The relationship between knowledge and values is a complicated one; the use of knowledge is, not surprisingly, subjective. It is much more likely that we will seek out knowledge retrospectively to justify our practice and decision-making, than that we will acquire knowledge beforehand, to inform our intervention. Social workers sometimes use selective knowledge to reinforce decisions that have already been reached, based on their belief system or value base (Brown, 1992b). This tendency has led to discriminatory practice (Brown, 1996).

'Social work knowledge', is a term used to cover quite different sets of material, and is an enormous and unwieldy entity. To make sense of this enormous and unwieldy entity, both here, and as a practitioner and as a manager supervising others, I organised relevant knowledge, that which is essential to practice, into three areas, while understanding that there are many other equally valid ways of so doing (Howe, 1987; Payne, 1991; Hanvey and Philpot, 1994):

> These three distinct areas are: knowledge that informs the practitioner about the client's experience and context; knowledge that helps the practitioner plan appropriate intervention; and knowledge that clarifies the practitioner's understanding of the legal, policy, procedural and organisational context in which their practice takes place. (Brown, 1996: 10)

It has been within the bodies of knowledge subsumed in the first two areas that the problematic ideas relating to lesbians and gay men have been found. The third area, covered partly in Chapter 3, has been problematic for different reasons, chiefly through social workers' lack of awareness of relevant matters. The first area, knowledge that informs the practitioner about the client's experience and context, draws on three academic perspectives; sociology, psychology and anti-discriminatory practice perspectives. The second area, knowledge that helps the practitioner plan appropriate intervention, covers methods and models of social work intervention and the theories that inform them. Bodies of knowledge that are covered in the third area are dependent on the national context in which social work practice takes place, and would relate to the major pieces of legislation directing social work assessment and the delivery of social work intervention and service delivery. The last area also needs to include legislation and policy that might be specific to particular service users or client groups, such as the material covered in Chapter 3.

To revisit knowledge that is relevant to the consideration of social work practice with lesbians and gay men, it will be necessary to focus on the first two areas outlined above. The problematic nature of the content of these two areas in relation to homosexuality has been in the form of both overtly discriminatory material and discrimination mostly by default and omission. However, within these areas there has also been the development of anti-discriminatory practice ideas relating specifically to lesbians and gay men. Relevant knowledge relating to particular areas of social work intervention and service delivery to adults in their own right, to adults in their capacity as carers of children, to children themselves and, lastly, to probation and offenders will be covered in Chapters 7, 8 and 9.

Theories, methods and models

Social work has a rich history of the integration of different, often conflicting, ideas about how intervention should be theorised, planned, executed and evaluated. The evolution of those ideas has often reflected social developments, and has sometimes developed as a reaction to previous social work orthodoxies. An outcome of this 'richness' is the range of ideas available to social workers to inform intervention: task-centred approaches, psychodynamic ideas, crisis intervention theory, systemic thinking, humanistic approaches, radical social work – the list is endless. It can be argued that the range of ideas available has led to the birth of a 'Jack and Jill of all trades, mistresses and masters of none'. However, diversity can also be a strength. 'Clients should be able to benefit from all available knowledge so theoretical perspectives should not be limited' (Payne, 1991: 51). Social work ideas are socially constructed; they are the product of a particular historical, economic, geographic and cultural moment. This means that, when we look to the usefulness of such ideas, we need to place them within their context of origin. We can then use them more effectively, neither assuming them to be universal truths nor throwing them out as non-specific to our own or our service users' immediate contexts.

Part of the process of professionalisation that social work has been engaged in, both in America and Britain, since the 1920s, has involved the search for an appropriate, relevant theoretical basis. This has been, at least in part, for the purpose of bolstering both its credibility and acceptability. From the 1930s onwards, with increasing enthusiasm, social work in Britain turned to psychoanalysis as a relevant body of ideas (Yelloly, 1980; Pearson, *et al.*, 1988). This was not at all surprising, because both psychoanalysis and social work, particularly from the 1940s, were addressing similar areas pertinent to direct work with clients and patients: attachment, loss, change and crisis. There developed an image of social work in this period that could be described as

> a profession of female social workers, which of course they were as indeed they still, primarily, are (Howe, 1986), calmly reflecting on the analytic process with their clients. (Brown, 1996: 11)

This description is then repudiated as

> something of a myth. Social work by its very nature has always had to have a significant element of pragmatism, involving itself as it has to, with the detail of peoples' day-to-day existence as well as their innermost feelings. Pearson *et al.* (1988) explain that the influence of psychoanalytic ideas in social work 'never even approached a psychoanalytic take-over; British social work was too firmly rooted in the Tawney tradition of democratic socialism

for that to be a possibility' (Pearson *et al.*, 1988: 4). (Brown, 1996: 11)

However, psychoanalytic ideas rather than psychoanalytic method were particularly and profoundly important in the development of social casework (Payne, 1992). The ways in which social work adopted psychoanalytic ideas were unfortunately often crude and simplistic, sometimes leading to prescriptive ways of working with complex human dilemmas. This simplistic adaptation had implications for the profession's approaches to lesbians and gay men. It is easy for us to forget the extraordinary discourses relating to gender and sexuality that were dominant in social work during that period. Wilson records the perspectives of one social work agency during the 1950s in Britain. She refers to a book edited by Pincus referring to work done by what was later renamed the Family Welfare Association:

The case histories in the body of the book are filled with amazing success stories, achieved through therapeutic casework, with women 'making astonishing moves towards femininity', and learning to become good mothers, and men rapidly overcoming their effeminacy and homosexual tendencies, achieving new status in work and doubling their earning capacities (see Weir, 1974). The authors stress the importance of correct gender identifications and the neurosis and immaturity to which those who fail to become truly 'masculine' or 'feminine' are condemned. Expressing the then current horror of homosexuality, the book expresses open disapproval of effeminate men or, even worse, of women such as Mrs P, 'a very hysterical girl, feminine in appearance but with an immense need to dominate and be masculine' or of Mrs M whose 'successful' treatment is described with naive brutality: 'The progress Mrs M made was obvious. She had gone a long way towards femininity; she showed a new interest in the home, in sewing and cooking. While . . . she seemed pleased about her achievements, she made angry remarks to the [social] worker, suggesting that she wanted to make her into a "humdrum housewife" with washing on Mondays, and a dull, competent routine' (Pincus 1953: 131). It is hard not to share Mrs M's suspicions. (Wilson, 1977: 87)

To be fair, it was not only social work's crude adaptation of psychoanalytic ideas, in relation to gender and sexuality, that was problematic, but it was also the body of ideas itself (Hart, 1980). Ryan and O'Connor, writing, in their important book about psychoanalysis today, note that:

> Psychoanalysis, as a body of theory and practice, has not been able to integrate homosexuality into itself. Instead, homosexuality remains largely split off, inadequately discussed and understood, subject to rigid and sometimes attacking theorising, and to excluding practices. Psychoanalytic theory, in many different ways . . . has seen all homosexuality as various forms of pathology, perversity or immaturity. (O'Connor and Ryan, 1993: 9)

Few would argue that psychoanalytic ideas have not been influential on social work theory and practice; the legacy of this for lesbian and gay men as social work clients/service users has not been helpful. The 1960s witnessed the demise of the dominant position of psychodynamic ideas in social work. However, they always remained the major theoretical perspective within particular agencies and for individuals within social work. Social work's rejection of psychoanalytic ideas and the psychodynamic approach is associated with a number of factors: the growing scepticism among social workers about the relevance of these ideas to the realities of a predominantly working class clientele; the individualistic nature of the approach which often ignored the context of people's lives; the lack of proven effectiveness of the approach; the uneconomic nature of long-term casework often associated with this approach and the rising respectability of other relevant academic disciplines, namely sociology and psychology, as well as the proliferation of different theories of social work intervention in the 1960s and 1970s. All these factors contributed to the demise of the dominance of psychoanalytic ideas in social work practice.

It is therefore somewhat ironic that during the demise of these ideas which had been used in non-facilitative ways with lesbians and gay men, there was simultaneously developing the seed of the reclamation of the psychodynamic approach as a tool for both understanding oppression and ways of overcoming it. Fanon was developing ideas around how psychoanalytic ideas could facilitate an understanding of Black oppression, and how Black people might be affected by racism, both emotionally and materially. He believed that, in order to move towards liberation, racism had to be fought externally but also from within the individual psyche, by examining how individuals had internalised or identified with oppressive ideas about themselves. Fanon's work has been immeasurably important in many ways and it paved the way for such ideas to be developed further in the following decades. PACE, a counselling service for lesbians and gay men, run by lesbians and gay men in London, uses psychoanalytic and psychodynamic ideas among others, in its work. These ideas have thus come full circle, from orthodoxy to rejection through to radical reappraisal and reclamation.

There have been many other theories, methods and models as well as those deriving from psychoanalytic ideas that have had an impact on social work's attitudes, beliefs and practice towards lesbians and gay men, but none has had an impact so profound. Other social work theories or models of intervention can be argued as being more neutral, such as the task-centred approach, because it is not developed from a set of ideas about human development or personality. Systems theory has been criticised for its normative approaches to families (Pilalis and Anderton, 1986), specifically in its ignoring of gender power relations. However, that has largely been redressed by the development of ideas that incorporate systemic thinking with gender-sensitive ideas (Perelberg and Miller, 1990; Burck and Speed, 1995). There is nothing, I would argue, inherently homophobic in systems theory as it has been applied to social work or in systemic family therapy. Where its application has been homophobic, it is more likely to be a reflection of the worker's value system impeding the work, rather than a reflection on the nature of the theoretical base.

Crisis intervention theory comprises another set of ideas that can be applied neutrally. However, crisis theory draws on ego psychology, and some of its exponents have been clear about their belief in the supremacy of heterosexuality as the only mature adult sexuality. Behavioural ideas and their application to social work clients and service users, particularly gay men, have been much more problematic (Christopher, 1987). Although the application of these behavioural interventions was not administered by social workers or to social work clients, it is likely that these practices did impact on the social work intervention. Historically it was in the area of aversion therapy, administered to gay men in psychiatric hospitals and prisons, that the material realities of oppressive beliefs were translated into barbaric acts. Hart describes how learning theory has been applied in group work, where boys whose behaviour is perceived as worrying because it might appear girl-like have their masculine behaviours positively reinforced (Hart, 1980: 59).

Theories, and the models and methods derived from them, may have been problematic historically in how they were applied to working with lesbians and gay men. Some of them may still be problematic, but the overriding factor that is likely to affect the service recipient is how any particular model, method or theory is applied. The application is likely to be affected by the beliefs, attitudes and values of the individual social workers and those of the particular agency. It would be as possible to take a 'neutral' approach, such as task-centred work, and still practice in an oppressive manner, as it would be possible to use psychodynamic ideas derived from psychoanalysis in a reflective and critical way, and offer intervention to lesbians and gay men that was neither oppressive nor discriminatory. Theories, methods and models are part of the package of knowledge that social workers need to help plan appropriate intervention. Such intervention needs to be facilitative and creative, not oppressive.

Psychology, sociology and radical social work

Psychology, sociology and radical social work have all contributed to there being a shift away from the heavy reliance on psychodynamic ideas in social work.

Radical social work, in the British context, can be seen as a bridge between the social casework approaches of the 1950s and 1960s and the development of anti-discriminatory practice as we now recognise it. The growth of sociology undoubtedly contributed to the creation of radical social work. Radical social work was critical of social work's lack of a political and social understanding of the position of the working class, and social work's relationship to it (Corrigan and Leonard, 1978).

The 'radical social work' tradition of the 1970s viewed the casework model as excessively individualistic and influenced by
pathological theories about the working class. However, radical
social work has itself often been criticised for neglecting the
specific experiences of women and black people, issues of homosexuality also remained marginal to its concerns. (Brown, 1992a:
204)

Marginal or not, the publications relevant to homosexuality that
emerged out of, or were helped to develop as a result of, changes
that radical social work contributed to, were highly significant and
remain so today. These included a chapter (Hart, 1980) that
appeared in Brake and Bailey's *Radical Social Work and Practice*
(1980), one of the major radical social work texts, and a book,
Theory and Practice of Homosexuality (Hart and Richardson, 1981).
Both made a significant contribution to locating social work's
difficulties with homosexuality within a social and political context.
These publications, however, are not rhetorical or blaming, but are
focused on practice and how to better it for lesbians and gay men.
The most recent radical social work text (Langan and Lee, 1989) did
not reflect this early interest of social work with sexual-orientation.
It was to be another ten years before there was another equivalent
publication (Brown, 1992a) in the British context. It is difficult to
measure the impact that the radical social work tradition had on
social work practice, but it did

> have an influence on the development of perspectives and ideas
> within social work theory and practice. It raised the awareness of
> class as a fundamentally important concept within social work. By
> its omission of race and gender, within its discourse (with some
> exceptions), it ironically made a contribution to the mushrooming
> of anti-discriminatory practice ideas in precisely those areas in the
> 1980s. (Brown, 1996: 12)

We will return to the development of anti-oppressive social work
ideas in the following section.

Sociology and psychology together comprise part of the knowledge base that I organise under 'knowledge that informs the practitioner about the client's experience and context'. Sociology
contributes to our understanding of context and offers us ways of

achieving such understanding, while psychology contributes to our understanding of individual, family and group experience. It is beyond the remit of this book to review sociology and psychology in the context of service delivery to lesbians and gay men, but it is relevant to note some general points. Much of our understanding of aspects of discrimination that directly impact on lesbians and gay men, such as oppression, labelling, stigmatisation and marginalisation, has been facilitated by sociological discourses. Mainstream sociology has not necessarily focused on homosexuality, but it has housed many academics who have made this their direct focus, such as Weeks (1995), McIntosh (1968), Plummer (1992) and Hart and Richardson (1981), to mention only a small selection. It is also relevant that many lesbian and gay studies courses have been developed under a sociological umbrella. However the sociology that most social workers are exposed to would not cover many of the texts mentioned above. Gagnon and Simon (1973) and Plummer (1975) made a considerable contribution to an understanding of the consequences of labelling sexually deviant behaviours. Along with others they were interested in the social construction of homosexuality, and the consequences of this construction for lesbians and gay men as well as for heterosexual men and women and for society as a whole.

These developments within sociological debates mirrored and were affected by some of the social and political processes involving lesbians and gay men during the same period. Individual sociologists have contributed a very great deal to our understandings of how homosexuality has been both understood and constructed. These understandings can help social workers in their attempts to contextualise their clients' experience, in relation to how those lesbians and gay men may be perceived and how that may then affect their perceptions of themselves. The location of sociological discourses surrounding homosexuality has shifted. The symbolic interactionists of the 1970s (Gagnon and Simon, 1973; Plummer, 1975), however marginal, were positioned within sociology. The lesbian and gay writing being developed more recently is likely to be found within the territory of lesbian and gay studies, which often brings together a whole range of disciplines; cultural studies, media studies, history, psychoanalysis, literature and sociology. This inclusion has strengthened the development of lesbian and gay studies within the academy, but it may also have diluted some of the mainstream sociological discussions that social workers might be exposed to.

Psychology holds a vast range of different perspectives within itself. It is possible to generalise and say that during their training, most social workers are exposed to two major bodies of psychological ideas: developmental psychology and abnormal psychology or psychopathology. These two 'umbrellas' comprise different theoretical approaches to the same phenomena, so that, for example, depression can be understood through learning theory perspectives or through those of psychoanalysis. Because the first umbrella, developmental psychology, is concerned with how human beings grow and develop, and the second is concerned with the 'abnormal', which homosexuality is often constructed as, psychology has made a considerable contribution to social workers' 'understandings' of lesbians and gay men. Psychoanalytic ideas, which have already been considered earlier in this chapter, set the scene for psychological perceptions of homosexuality. The development of ego psychology, which was particularly prevalent in America, has made a strong contribution to understandings of how human beings develop from babyhood to old age. The other major contributions that have impacted on social work are the ideas arising out of the British school of object relations. The major proponent of ego psychology, who had a profound impact on social work education, was Erikson (1965). Although social workers are now exposed to many more ideas, Erikson's life cycle approach to development still holds tremendous influence in people's minds. Within his sixth stage of development, which he describes as 'intimacy versus isolation' covering the period of young adulthood, he comments on genitality and sex, describing the ideal as:

> mutuality of orgasm, with a loved partner, of the other sex, with whom one is able to share a mutual trust, and with whom one is able and willing to regulate the cycles of work, procreation and recreation so as to secure to the offspring, too, all the stages of a satisfactory development. (Erikson, 1965: 257, quoted in Gibson, 1991: 44)

Gibson comments that 'such a definition raises all kinds of issues, not least about the relative importance of orgasm, heterosexual love and procreation' (1991: 44). The 'normal' development that Erikson is describing is heterosexual: homosexuals need not apply.

Within the British school of object relations there have been many individuals whose work has been influential, including Fairbairn and Winnicott. Gibson describes Fairbairn's definition of 'mature dependency' (Fairbairn, 1952) as a healthy adult intimate relationship, being:

> based on a capacity to put something of oneself into a relationship and to accept something back from the other person, based on an acceptance in reality of each other as individuals. This requires a degree of trust in others, a sense of autonomy in self and a mature attitude to unresolved parent/child issues. (Gibson, 1991: 44)

Homosexuals may apply. There is nothing in this rather wonderful definition of mature dependency that would debar an individual lesbian or gay man. This may, however, not have been Fairbairn's explicit intention, writing, as he was, in the early 1950s. Many analysts who wrote about intimacy, attachment, mothering and separation during this period are dismissed as normative and prescriptive, and the conclusion is drawn that their ideas are, therefore, oppressive. However, to dismiss the work of such great thinkers and practitioners, as, for example, Fairbairn (1952), Winnicott (1986, 1988) and Bowlby (1988) for such reasons would be ignorant and detrimental ultimately to service users. (I include Bowlby in this context, although he is not considered to be part of the school of object relations, but, rather, to reside slightly outside it. He has, however, made a highly significant contribution to social work thinking in the areas of attachment and loss, and must surely figure as one of the contributors to this area, although it has become fashionable to ridicule and dismiss his work on highly spurious grounds.) When we study any text we must locate it within its historical, cultural, economic and geographical context to be able to assess its usefulness today to our specific practice experience. To suggest that ideas around intimacy, attachment, mothering and separation are not relevant to lesbians and gay men would be dehumanising. A more recent text, much used on social work courses, includes the following contextualisation in its chapter on partnership and marriage:

> We will be concerned primarily with heterosexual partners, but a reader can easily extrapolate those aspects which could equally apply to homosexual partners living together. (Rayner, 1986: 188)

Most of the writing arising out of psychoanalytic contributions to developmental psychology has assumed a particular construction of heterosexuality, but that does not mean that it is impossible to extrapolate material and ideas that are equally relevant to lesbians and gay men, who are, after all, just ordinary, complex human beings.

Within the area of psychopathology, social work teaching has relied more heavily on behavioural psychology and psychiatry, neither of which have historically viewed homosexuality as anything other than pathology. Homosexuality within this area would have been studied as an aspect of the abnormal, the gone-very-wrong. Until recently, homosexuality was defined as a mental disorder. In addition, social work texts dealing with the areas of psychiatry and mental disorder included such comments as 'Most lesbians are content to keep their homosexual inclinations hidden from general view and it is only the most psychopathic among them who make a show of their abnormality' (Munro and McCulloch, 1969: 157). Mental illness or abnormal psychology will be revisited in Chapter 8.

In response to the marginalisation or pathologicalisation of homosexuality within mainstream psychology, there has developed a literature of alternative discourses. These have not just been in relation to homosexuality but have developed in relation to Black perspectives and women. Such publications relating to lesbians and gay men would include the Boston Lesbian Psychologies Collective (1987), Gonsiorek and Weinrich (1991), Bozett and Sussman (1990), Bozett (1989a), Greene and Herek (1994) and Kitzinger (1987). It is noteworthy that the vast majority of these publications are American.

For social work practitioners to fully utilise available knowledge to facilitate an understanding of their clients/service users' experience and context they need to critically evaluate relevant sociological and psychological perspectives, placing those perspectives within their historical, cultural, economic and geographical contexts. In addition, they need to develop an awareness of relevant literature that relates specifically to lesbians and gay men which lies slightly or completely outside the mainstream.

Anti-oppressive/anti-discriminatory practice literature

One of the ironies about the relationship between radical social work and anti-oppressive/anti-discriminatory practice literature is that radical social work's omissions of, particularly, race and gender (with notable exceptions) within its discourses, unwittingly contributed to developments in those areas. Radical social work most importantly raised the awareness of class as a fundamentally important concept within social work:

> It is noteworthy that in the 1990s we have feminist social work knowledge and practice (Hanmer and Statham, 1988; Dominelli and McLeod, 1989; Langan and Day, 1992), and anti-racist social work (Ahmad, 1990; Dominelli, 1988; Husband, 1991; Hutchinson-Reis, 1989) but no equivalent body in relation to class. (Brown, 1996: 13)

It is also noteworthy that there has been very little development of writing in relation to social work with lesbians and gay men either. Feminist social work literature might have been expected to have made a contribution to thinking around lesbians and social work, but in the main that has not been the case. Brown comments:

> Recent feminist social work literature has had little, beyond generalities, to say about lesbians (Brook and Davis, 1985; Dale and Foster, 1986: Hanmer and Statham, 1988). There is little appreciation that lesbians are as diverse as heterosexual women, the only commonality being their oppression as lesbians . . . Although Dominelli and McLeod only briefly touch on lesbianism, they do recognise the diversities and complexities among lesbians (Dominelli and McLeod, 1989). However, in presenting a positive perspective on lesbians, they end up with a rather romanticised view of reality; 'For feminists, lesbianism is no longer lodged in the realms of the psychopathological and has been increasingly recognised and legitimated as an intensely

expressive form of relationship in its own right by substantial numbers of women within the women's movement' (Dominelli and McLeod, 88). (Brown, 1992: 204a)

One of the major contributions that radical social work did make was precisely within this area, already discussed earlier in this chapter. Within what can be described as the anti-discriminatory/ anti-oppressive social work literature, there have been few relevant publications in Britain, other than Brown (1991), Brown (1992a), Buckley (1992), McCaughey and Buckley (1993), Thompson (1993), Thompson (1994), Denney (1996) and Logan *et al.* (1996). Some important contributions have probably been omitted, but there have only been two major texts solely dealing with this area, namely McCaughey and Buckley (1993) and Logan *et al.* (1996). The picture is somewhat different in the American context. Not only is there considerable material within the area of psychology that is specifically related to lesbians and gay men, but there are main texts about generic social work with lesbians and gay men (Kus, 1990a; Woodman, 1992), as well as numerous texts relating to particular areas of specialism within social work practice (for example, childcare) that have a lesbian and gay focus (this will be considered in Chapters 7 and 8).

To be fully able to contextualise a client's or service user's experience, relevant anti-discriminatory/anti-oppressive practice literature needs to be drawn on. Practitioners in the British context, when considering practice with lesbians and gay men, as well as being familiar with the British material will also need to draw on texts from America.

Utilising knowledge effectively

This chapter has outlined some of the problematic issues in informing competent practice with appropriate knowledge, when working with lesbians and gay men. We can see that knowledge that is drawn on to inform the practitioner about the client/service user's experience and context, and knowledge that helps the practitioner to plan appropriate intervention, throw up many difficulties when we come to apply this knowledge to lesbians and gay men. In practice and within social work education I have found this situation is manageable if we apply two very basic principles. First, all knowledge drawn upon needs to be critically evaluated and contextualised. Second, specific knowledge within a particular area of practice that directly addresses the lives of lesbians and gay men needs to be sought out. This then means that the practitioner can be as well informed as possible before engaging with service users. No knowledge ever allows us to 'know' another's experience, but it does enable the practitioner to engage, in a more informed way. The only way of really 'knowing' another's experience is by asking them. How we ask them will be affected by the knowledge we have access to and how we have made use of it.

The development of anti-oppressive perspectives in social work has sometimes been associated with didactic pronouncements, certainty, apportioning blame and the assumption of the superiority of the 'correct'. This does not equate with good practice. When practitioners approach knowledge, it needs to be with an enquiring, open mind that is able to tolerate ambiguity and uncertainty. This approach is needed to enable clients/service users and practitioners to benefit from the full range of knowledge available to them, to enable the most appropriate service or intervention to be the outcome.

6

Social Work: Organisation and Context

Social work is a varied activity that takes place in an increasing number of different contexts. The organisation of its delivery in these different contexts is subject to central government directives as well as local negotiation. The organisation of social work delivery is a dynamic entity. The degree of reorganisations that social services have undergone in Britain can be understood as a sometimes dysfunctional way of attempting to manage too many imposed changes that have generated intolerable anxiety on both individuals within Social Services Departments or Social Services Departments as organisations (Brown and Pearce, 1992). If we are to talk about social work with lesbians and gay men, we must accept that what we say has to be contextualised in relation to the organisational setting at the point of delivery. For example, what might need to be considered if the setting were a child protection agency will differ from the considerations necessary in a probation hostel, which would be different again from those that would be relevant to a hospice. It will not be possible to examine every organisational context, but it is possible to address themes which may be relevant to all organisations, irrespective of their specific functions. These would include autonomous organisation versus integration, supervision, assessment, and service provision.

Autonomous organisation versus integration

In Chapter 4 it was suggested that there may be a link between the security and open inclusion of lesbians and gay men in social work organisations and the quality of the experience for lesbian and gay clients/service users as consumers of those organisations interventions and services. The security and feeling of inclusion will need to be backed by protective employment policies, partly because of the lack of any legal employment rights for lesbians and gay men. There has always been the question hovering over social work provision of whether or not it is realistic to expect the mainstream provision of services to ever adequately assess the needs of oppressed groups and be able to offer an appropriate provision to meet them. Dalrymple and Burke point out the loaded power relationship between the provider and the provided for. Discussing Zarb's work (1991) addressing assessment in relation to people who are ageing with a disability, they write:

> assessment reflects the power relationships between professionals and disabled people. This means that it is the professionals who define and assess the needs, rather than allowing disabled people to define their own needs. He argues, therefore, that people with disabilities are unable to retain control over how they may wish to live (Dalrymple and Burke, 1995: 114)

Although this reference is specific to disabled people, it also has general applicability to other oppressed groups. One important point raised by Zarb is that by engaging with a social work agency you may lose your autonomy, your right to define your own needs and the possibility of maintaining control over your life in important areas. Empowerment and partnership are concepts that have become popular and accepted currency within social work practice. These two terms are meant to mitigate against feelings of powerlessness and loss of autonomy. However, although these two concepts have been absorbed into the orthodox discourses of social work (Baistow, 1995), it is difficult to know what real impact this has had on service recipients. Lesbians and gay men have sometimes opted for separate autonomous organisation for the provision of services as the only way they have felt it would be possible to retain their individual and group autonomy, define their own needs, and maintain control over important areas of their own lives. The development of such autonomous organisations has also been in response to the failure of mainstream social work organisations to provide an adequate service or providing no service at all:

It is ideal to have lesbian women and gay men use agencies and programs that exist to serve the whole community. Social workers have a responsibility to work towards this ideal. The reality is, however, that many resources either do not have the necessary knowledge or skills or do not operate from a value perspective that is helpful in serving lesbian women and gay men. (Burnham, 1992)

Within the British context, the setting up of the Albert Kennedy Trust and the Gay Bereavement Project would be examples of two such autonomous organisations.

The Albert Kennedy Trust was set up in response to the tragic death, at the age of sixteen, of Albert Kennedy, a runaway from the care system, his death being attributed in part to the homophobia he experienced. The Trust's mission is to ensure that all young lesbian and gay men are able to live in accepting, supportive and caring homes. Their aims are:

To improve attitudes within society towards lesbian and gay young people; to promote greater understanding of lesbian and gay young people wherever they live and to provide accepting, supportive and caring homes for lesbian and gay people who would otherwise be homeless or in a hostile environment. (Albert Kennedy Trust, 1995: 3)

The main bulk of the Trust's work is the recruitment of supportive placements for lesbian and gay young people over sixteen and working, in conjunction with social services departments, with young people who are under sixteen. The Trust covers the Manchester and Greater London areas, meeting a need that up until 1989 remained publicly unspoken, causing terrible suffering and unacceptable consequences for large numbers of young people, and which took the death of Albert Kennedy to make public.

It was an organisation set up in the form of a trust that tried to redress the problem, not the statutory services. The relationship between autonomous provision and the mainstream is complex. There are two main arguments in relation to the impact of voluntary, autonomous organisations on statutory services. The first is that if separate provision is made to meet a particular need, as with the Albert Kennedy Trust, then the statutory services can effectively wash their hands of their obligation to provide such a service themselves. The second, contradictory, argument is that, when a voluntary agency begins to address a particular need, this raises the awareness of mainstream organisations who respond by considering those needs themselves. The Albert Kennedy Trust has raised the awareness of the unmet needs of young lesbians and gay men both generally and also, in particular, with social services departments, especially in relation to young people for whom local authorities are responsible:

> The Albert Kennedy Trust has brought the problems faced by gay and lesbian youngsters into sharp relief. (M. T. Head, The Children's Society, quoted in Albert Kennedy Trust, 1995: 7)

Another organisation set up outside mainstream provision to meet an unspoken, unseen and unmet need, was the Gay Bereavement Project. The project was initially set up to offer a round-the-clock telephone counselling service. Because of the often invisible nature of lesbian and gay relationships, death and bereavement can pose difficulties over and above those usually encountered. The death of a partner may be unacknowledged, even unrecognised, as the couple may never have made their relationship known, for fear of homophobic responses. The birth families of the bereaved may exclude the partner:

> For some people, problems with the family start with the funeral arrangements. Parents may be worried about what other family members will think if they find out the dead person was gay and the chief mourner turns out to be gay too. (Wertheimer, 1987: 9)

As with the Albert Kennedy Trust, a need that may well have been assumed to be met by mainstream organisations offering bereavement counselling had remained unmet. Woodman discusses the development of social work organisations in America set up specifically to meet the needs of lesbian and gay communities. She describes one such organisation in New York:

> A lesbian and gay service centre has been established in New York City. It houses a wide range of social, recreational, legal, and social services programs. The building symbolises the growth of

one community's services. The New York City centre represents
the broadest usage of the notion of social welfare. Although not
all of New York City's services to lesbians and gays are housed in
this space, examples to be found there include: services to the
elderly, support groups, recreational associations, political organisations, social groups, counselling, ethnic orientated organisations, hot lines, physically challenged, music, sports, religion,
sexual minorities and archives. (Woodman, 1992: 194)

Despite the different cultural context and the vast differences
between America and Britain in how the provision of welfare has
been organised in the past and is organised now, we can see that
Britain still has some way to go to even begin to address the welfare
needs of its lesbian and gay communities.

The setting up of separate organisations to meet the social work
and welfare needs of lesbians and gay men has happened partly as a
response to those needs remaining unacknowledged, and/or unmet,
by the mainstream social work organisations, within both the
voluntary and the statutory sectors. They have also been set up
because they can make sure that they have an ethic of acceptance
and a purpose to provide positive services to lesbians and gay men
(Klein, 1990: 315). The contexts that social work takes place in, and
the organisations that offer that social work, often lack that ethic.

The setting up and running of agencies designed to meet the needs
of lesbians and gay men both accomplish the aim of providing an
appropriate provision and raise the possibility of the acknowledgement of the unmet needs of lesbians and gay communities and
individuals by the mainstream social work organisations. However,
the provision of services to the lesbian and gay communities by
autonomous organisations does not provide all the answers. There
will always be needs that have to be met by the mainstream agencies,
and lesbians and gay men should have the same right of access to
appropriate and sensitive services within the mainstream as other
clients and service users have. Some lesbians and gay men can
choose the organisation they may want to approach to access a
particular service, but many do not. A large proportion of social
work clients/service users are not choosing to be in that role. They
are clients/service users because they have no choice. The incorpora-
tion of language which apparently includes concepts such as empowerment and partnership into orthodox social work discourses

sometimes disguises the glossing over of this reality. For example, such euphemistic language as service user, which tries to convey notions of partnership and consumerism together with an assumption of choice, is both patronising and insulting when used to describe a person being admitted to hospital by ambulance, with a police presence, under a section of the Mental Health Act 1983.

Lesbians and gay men, like heterosexual men and women, are often in contact with social work organisations because they have no choice. They may be parents involved in a child protection investigation, offenders on probation orders, young people being accommodated by a local authority, patients in a psychiatric hospital, a person recovering from a road accident to discover that one of their legs has been amputated, a carer of a person described as elderly mentally infirm, or an individual in residential care dependent on others as a result of a debilitating stroke. These are the people who often do not have the choice to seek out social work provision that is specifically designed to meet the needs of lesbians and gay men.

Social work organisations have both a moral and a statutory responsibility, within some areas of provision, to meet the needs of all clients/service users with sensitive and appropriate services. For many social work organisations, offering a sensitive and appropriate service necessitates a considerable examination of the ways their provision is organised. Areas worth identifying, relevant to all social work organisational contexts are:

1. Open respect for and inclusion of lesbian and gay staff, backed by equal opportunities policies covering employment rights and harassment.
2. Respect for and the valuing of diversity.
3. Welcome. Welcoming is an essential part of the engagement process for clients/service users, which is conveyed through physical and material media as well as interpersonally. If, as a service user, I arrive at an agency that conveys the message that I am unwanted and potentially violent, by the physical barriers I am required to transcend, including having to enter via security doors and talk to the receptionist through a grill, I am unlikely to feel welcome. This may affect my initial willingness to engage. For lesbians and gay men, who may feel anxious about engaging with an agency that they might assume to be hostile towards homosexuality, this lack of welcome may increase their anxiety.

4. Images. There was much controversy surrounding the London
    Borough of Haringey (Cooper, 1994), in the late 1980s, about
    the Borough's wish to convey positive images of lesbians and
    gay men. Organisations do not have to convey positive images,
    but they do need to consider the images they do convey and
    whether or not these images are excluding or including of the
    diversity of their clientele.
5. Language. The words we use convey our assumptive worlds.
    Social work organisations need to consider their assumptive
    worlds and how these are conveyed in written and verbal forms.
    The use of language has been and still is a powerful medium for
    heterosexist assumptions.
6. Interactive dynamism. Social work is an interactive process
    which has to be responsive and dynamic. Social work organisa-
    tions need to reflect this by being not only responsive, willing to
    and able to change, but also able to reflect on their intervention
    and provision. Quality assurance needs to involve the active
    participation of clients/service users to be effective.

Reviewing the ways in which social work provision is organised and
delivered to lesbians and gay men means that there are potential
benefits for everyone. It would be rare to find an agency that was
not addressing the above points but was offering a good enough
service to any of its clients/service users, not only lesbians and gay
men. There will always be the need and the desire for autonomous
organisations that provide services specifically for the lesbian and
gay communities and lesbian and gay individuals. While this will
remain the case, there will still be a significant number of lesbians
and gay men who either choose to use, or have no option but to use,
the mainstream social work organisations. These individuals have
the right to an inclusive, welcoming, respectful and competent
provision.

Supervision

Supervision of social workers is a requirement in the majority of
social work contexts, or at least it is seen as desirable. It is the
organisation that is responsible through its management structures
to make sure it happens, if that organisation deems it necessary.

Supervision has many functions and, in relation to the quality of social work intervention, these were specified in the Beckford report as:

> To ensure that the social worker has the knowledge and skills to carry out her task . . .
> To monitor the activities of the social worker . . .
> To be aware of the attitudes of the social worker towards the case and to correct, if necessary, the way in which they affect her handling of it . . .
> To support the social worker both practically and emotionally. (London Borough of Brent, 1985: 215–17)

Supervision is also one of the vehicles through which social work organisations transmit their cultures and control their workforces.

Marny, in a text examining sexuality and organisations, refers to the antagonism between homosexuality and organisations (Hall, 1989: 126). Lesbians and gay men often experience this antagonism via the supervisory process. This is most likely to be the case if the organisation lacks a culture that fosters acceptance, respect and the valuing of difference, or where the supervisor generally lacks competence and compensates for this through over-directive and controlling ways of supervising staff, or is personally anxious in the face of homosexuality. Supervision in social work is a very private affair and, unlike some other areas, it has rarely been opened up for scrutiny and evaluation through the processes of quality assurance. Hart argues that lesbian and gay social workers pose a threat to an accepted aspect of social work culture itself:

> Openly gay social workers . . . do pose a threat – to theories of sexual pathology and corruption, of gender role and family life, and perhaps most important, to the distance placed between helper and helped in social work's professional culture. (Hart, 1980: 46)

Lesbian and gay workers are sometimes accused, within the supervisory process, of possible over-identification with lesbian or gay clients. Within social services, I have experienced a lesbian social worker's work being monitored in this respect, in a way that would have been unthinkable had it been a heterosexual worker with a heterosexual client. Of course, one of the tasks of the supervisor is to help the social worker maintain appropriate objectivity, but if this objectivity is pursued in a single-minded fashion only in one area, then it is likely to be about sustaining the marginality of lesbians and gay men, workers or clients, at the edges of the organisation. There is a professional tension for social work that is often made concrete within the supervisory process – the tension between professional autonomy and organisational control. It may also be the context where individuals experience some ambivalence and tension between social work as a profession and social work as a possible social and political activity:

> Indeed, some social workers are against professionalisation, thinking that it means becoming part of the establishment, and distances worker and client, making the latter dependent and subservient. (Coulshed, 1990: 130)

Supervision is the organisational context where individual workers have to account for their activities and be accountable. This is important to safeguard clients'/service users' best interests. This function of accountability should not be confused with control or the maintenance of a particular heterosexual *status quo*.

Hawkins and Shohet (1989), using Winnicott's concept of the good enough mother, develop this idea within the supervisory context. They argue that the supervisory relationship needs to be a place where the disturbance generated and experienced through direct work can be appropriately contained and held, in order for this not to destroy the worker. Good enough supervision is necessary in social work as the nature of the work is often of a most disturbing nature. Within the context of this chapter, it is pertinent in two areas. First, for lesbians and gay men, there may be complex issues provoked by working with lesbians and gay men that cannot be subsumed under a simplistic heading like over-identification. All lesbians and gay men, irrespective of whether or not they are social workers or clients/service users, are at the receiving end of oppressive ideologies and behaviours, although they will have individual ways of both experiencing and perceiving that oppression. This shared reality means there may well be some identification with the client/service user. This possible identification can be disturbing to the worker and needs to be openly explored within supervision.

Unless this happens, in my experience in the role of social worker and supervisor of lesbian and gay staff, the 'fallout' tends to be either a lack of objectivity or a response of 'over-distancing'. The first response manifests itself by the worker sympathising with the client/service user to the extent that the presenting behaviour, which may be unacceptable, such as child abuse, is understood through the prism of heterosexism alone. Although heterosexism and homophobia as forms of oppression are powerful forces, they can only be understood in terms of additional 'vulnerability' factors impacting on individuals, not as the sole cause of a person's difficulties. The second response, the 'over-distancing', often manifests itself in either a collusion with a particular member of the client/service users system, other than the lesbian or gay person, as a defence against that particular pairing, or the development of hostility towards the lesbian or gay client/service user. Difficult emotional reactions can be experienced by lesbians and gay men working in a helping capacity with lesbians and gay men who may be distressed or indeed 'disturbed'. Such a situation can restimulate all the workers own fears of homosexuality being either pathological or perceived as pathological. Much of the campaigning around the rights of lesbians and gay men has been on the basis of lesbians and gay men being 'normal' but different in relation to their sexual orientation. Distressed lesbians and gay men, needing intervention, particularly where this is statutory intervention, can be perceived as 'gone wrong', and the lesbian or gay social worker, either at a conscious or, more usually, an unconscious level, may want to distance themselves from such a manifestation.

Social work clients/service users who are in conflict with a social work agency or social worker will often emotionally attack points of vulnerability they perceive within the worker, for reasons which are important for psychological survival. Lesbians and gay social workers sometimes fear this attack will be focused on their homosexuality, although in my experience this has never been the case with out social workers, who are confident of the support of both their agency and their supervisor. However, where it does occur, the fear of this possible exposure or attack is very real and needs to be heard. To fully support lesbian and gay social workers and safeguard clients/service users' best interests, there has to be good-enough supervision available. The areas mentioned above are, in practice, highly complex, and can only be appropriately worked through within a trusting, competent, accepting and reflective supervisory relationship. To work with such issues within a supervisory relationship that lacks these components may well be experienced by the social worker as a homophobic attack, which, in reality, is sometimes precisely what it is.

For all social workers, irrespective of their sexuality, working with lesbian and gay clients/service users provokes complex issues. These issues are also pertinent to working around other areas of oppression. One major theme that emerges is the need to differentiate between the oppression itself and its consequences for the individual. The complexity arises because, in reality, oppression and its consequences are utterly interrelated and cannot be separated out. However, there has been a tendency in social work in the recent past to distil an understanding of the difficulties a person may be experiencing purely down to the oppression they experience. Oppression contributes to a situation, but it is rarely the whole explanation. Where social work has historically pathologised a particular group, one of the unhelpful reactions to this has been the romanticisation of such oppressed groups. The move from negative to positive stereotyping, which is, in either case, still stereotyping, is an aspect of this. An elaboration of this process has been articulated in the field of child protection and its complex interrelationship with racism:

> The dangers of negative and positive stereotyping have been excellently demonstrated in the Tyra Henry inquiry (London Borough of Lambeth, 1987). The inquiry describes how the black Afro-Caribbean grandmother was seen as a type, a positive stereotype of an all-coping indestructible matriarch, not as an individual. (Brown, 1992a: 216)

Supervision is the context in which the social work organisation concentrates its own responsibility to hold social workers accountable for their work, and to facilitate good enough work being undertaken with clients/service users. It is the organisation's responsibility to make sure the quality of the supervision is 'good enough'.

Assessment

Assessment is neither organisation nor context. It is, however, increasingly the context through which the public make contact with or are processed through social work organisations. Assessment throws up generic areas relevant to the following three chapters, and although assessment will be returned to within those chapters, it is worth noting some general points here.

Coulshed describes assessment as:

> an ongoing process, in which the client participates, whose purpose is to understand people in relation to their environment; it is a basis for planning what needs to be done to maintain, improve or bring about change in the person, the environment or both. (Coulshed, 1991: 24)

The key words here seem to be ongoing, participates, understand people in relation to their environment, and planning. Assessment, then, needs to be a joint venture, the social worker and the client/service user together trying to understand the situation. Assessments can be grouped as types under four headings: assessments of need, assessments of risk, assessments of prospective carers and assessments of offending behaviours. In the British context these headings correspond to particular pieces of legislation, which will be explored in Chapters 7, 8 and 9.

Smale *et al.* identify three approaches to assessment: the questioning model, the exchange model and the procedural model:

> In the questioning model the professional is assumed to be the expert in identifying need. In the procedural model, a variation of the questioning model, it is assumed that the managers drawing up guidelines for workers have expertise in setting the criteria for resource allocation. To this extent they are the experts in how problems should be managed and resources allocated. In the exchange model, it is assumed that the clients and other people in the situation, and the professional, all have equally valid perceptions of the problems and can contribute to their solution or perpetuation. (Smale *et al.*, 1993: 7)

The exchange model would seem to be the most appropriate to fit Coulshed's description of assessment, and the most appropriate when undertaking an assessment involving lesbians and gay men. To undertake a competent assessment social workers need to keep in mind the following:

1. *Awareness and containment of their own assumptive world.* This means understanding that their beliefs, attitudes and values are specific to them and may not be shared by others, and should not cloud an assessment or impact inappropriately on the process.

2. *Development of anti-oppressive practice.* This would include the above, as well as working in partnership, to facilitate empowerment.

3. *Risk.* Many assessments are about the assessment of risk. The identification of the person with least power in a given situation is a component of this, and is not always obvious. Risk assessment has to take precedence over any other considerations; other factors can be considered at a later stage.

4. *Material circumstances.* Poverty is the overriding condition that many clients/service users have to contend with. Even if it cannot be alleviated, it has to be acknowledged.

5. *Emotional realities/perceptions.* This is the feelings aspect of assessment. Different people feel differently about the same situations and individuals within the same system may experience the same event in quite varied ways.

6. *The individual must be viewed within their own group/context and community.* Community here refers to two meanings of the term; first, geographical neighbourhood and second, community of interest, for example lesbian and gay communities that may transcend geographical boundaries.

7. *Assessment of the immediate system.* This is not necessarily only those living under a single roof, and needs to involve all significant others.

8. *Care planning.* The joint assessment needs to be followed by joint care planning, not necessarily undertaken by the same person, but underpinned by the same principles of partnership and empowerment.

9. *Review.* Peoples lives and circumstances are dynamic and continually changing. This means that the care plan must be constantly reviewed and the ways in which it has been implemented regularly evaluated and reassessed.

These nine points of assessment are crucial, irrespective of whether the assessment is of need, risk, offending behaviours or prospective carers.

Assessment is often the first point at which clients/service users actually meet a representative of the social work organisation. The social worker is having to assess a situation that is unique and sometimes unfamiliar. Working with lesbians and gay men does, for many social workers, feel unfamiliar and when social workers are confronted with working with difference (and, indeed, sameness), it is important that they are able to keep certain aspects that are integral to discrimination in mind:

Oppression: material
                 social
                 emotional
Stereotyping: positive
                 negative
Invisibility
Label as a generalised focus
Paternalism
Interrelationship of different structural oppressions

The first aspect, oppression, is broken down into three areas as it impacts on individuals in these ways, affecting their material circumstances, their social interactions and their emotional well-being.

We need to guard against stereotyping of any sort, because it reduces individuals to types and is dehumanising.

Invisibility operates in this context in a number of ways. The needs of individuals and communities may remain invisible because they are not recognised, as is often the case with lesbians and gay men. A person's sexual orientation is not visible and should not be assumed.

'Label as a generalised focus' is where the worker just sees the label and fails to see the person. This is particularly pertinent to lesbians and gay men whose sexuality can become obsessively focused upon, to the exclusion of the complexity of their lives and who they are as complete human beings.

Paternalism is a powerful aspect of oppression. Speaking for, protecting and knowing better than the individual concerned are all behaviours which infantilise, and although people may well need support in dealing with, for example, harassment, they need to be heard and to be facilitated to draw on or develop their own skills to confront and survive such behaviours. To undertake a competent assessment with lesbians or gay men, to really develop an understanding of the unique individual within their own context, requires the above to be held in mind.

Different social work contexts

Social work takes place in many different contexts and settings. Some of these have a primary social work function, but in other contexts and settings the social work aspect may be peripheral to the primary tasks of the organisation. For example, the role of the social worker in the accident and emergency department of a general hospital has to be secondary to the primary function of saving lives. This section could be never-ending, but I have chosen to briefly look at four areas: multidisciplinary work, day care settings, residential settings and outreach work.

Social work is often one dimension of a multidisciplinary approach. This approach is sometimes actualised through the formation of teams. Ovretveit offers a general definition of a multidisciplinary team as

> a group of practitioners with different professional training (multidisciplinary), employed by more than one agency (multi-agency), who meet regularly to co-ordinate their work providing services to one or more clients in a defined area. (Øvretveit, 1993: 9)

Social workers have had to take on the complexities and the potential richness of multidisciplinary work, having increasingly been directed by legislation to do so (Department of Health, 1991e, 1996). Social work has always been part of a multidisciplinary approach in many contexts, the almoner being an early example. One important change since the almoner has been the development of an expectation, not always realised, that there will be a change in power relationships in multidisciplinary teams, a shift to the extent of each participating discipline being equal but different, contributing their own area of expertise. One significant area of difference that can be relevant in work with lesbians and gay men is that professional groups are exposed to very different trainings and policies within their own professions or organisations. This can become apparent in the arena of anti-oppressive practice. Social workers may have had to focus in their training on their own values, beliefs and attitudes, but other professional trainings may not have given this area the same emphasis. Attitudes vary between professionals regarding the validity of homosexuality, though it would be inaccurate to typecast any particular professional group. Social work can make a specific contribution to multidisciplinary teams and approaches by contributing possible understandings around the development of anti-oppressive practice.

A significant number of preventative resources operate in the organisational context of day centres. Accessing these preventative resources for certain groups has been of concern. Particularly in relation to Black communities, social workers have been shown to perceive there to be a link between inaccessibility to preventative services and compulsory admission to hospital:

> Of greater concern was the feeling that preventative mental health services are not accessible enough to black people and that this results in people being referred later in the development of their problems. (Bowl and Barnes, 1990: 13)

The reasons for such inaccessibility are many. For instance, an individual's feelings of alienation may be considerably exacerbated when that person is placed in a setting that seemingly has a dominant homogeneous cultural norm, in relation to which they are, or perceive themselves to be, outsiders. Earlier in this chapter, six areas were identified for consideration as to how an organisation may consider its service delivery. These areas are especially important in day care settings. Unless these factors are reflected upon, it is likely that lesbians and gay men will absent themselves, if they are referred to a day care resource in a voluntary capacity or where they are in a position to resist. Some preventative day centres are not entirely voluntary, day facilities for young offenders being one example. I have been involved in two London boroughs running training for intermediate treatment workers, to examine how the organisations are experienced from the perspective of young lesbians and gay men. There is evidence to suggest that this client group may be particularly vulnerable on a number of counts (Trenchard and Warren, 1984), those who are already engaged with the criminal justice system being a particular case in point. The areas that seemed to carry most significance, identified from the factors needing consideration by agencies, were the use of inclusive and exclusive language and how welcome individuals felt.

Residential settings are places where people live – their homes – where they should be able to express every aspect of themselves, including their wishes regarding their intimate sexual behaviours and attachments. Realising people's right to the expression of their sexually active selves is a complex issue in residential settings, given that many people are living in close proximity. Many establishments have relied on the maximisation of the use of public space and the lack of respect and valuing of private space. Sexual activity for most of us is associated with the use of this private space. Sex is a controversial issue in many residential organisations but, despite it provoking much anxiety among workers and absorbing much time, Parkin points out that despite the fact that

> sexuality is an ever-present issue for workers and residents within residential care organisations, . . . it is notably absent from staff meeting agendas, training programmes, organisational policies, rules and guidelines. (Parkin, 1989: 110)

This vacuum relates to all sexual activity, heterosexual or homosexual. However homosexual sex does, in certain settings, provoke extreme anxiety on the behalf of workers, especially in settings for young people. There can also be dynamics in probation settings that may be relevant to other contexts. Lloyd, writing about the position of lesbian and gay clients in residential probation settings, states that

> the experience of both men and women indicated two main things. First, people who are physically or mentally powerful can transcend their disadvantaged status, especially if they are prepared to bully. Second, attitudes of the staff team are critical in the production of an atmosphere free from harassment on whatever grounds, and these need the backing of policy. (Lloyd, 1993: 41)

'Home' has many functions, one being the fuelling of ourselves, emotionally as well as physically. To do this we must be able to be true to ourselves. The consequences for lesbians and gay men, who may feel they either cannot 'be themselves' or who have to hide part of who they are, are likely to be emotionally damaging. In filling the organisational vacuum in relation to sex and sexuality generally, we must beware of privileging one sexuality above another.

In order that social work agencies may remain effective, they need to be in communication with and informed by lesbian and gay resources and organisations, so as to be able to work from a better knowledge base. Outreach work means many different things. It can simply mean the above, making sure that social work organisations stay in close contact with autonomous lesbian and gay organisations.

Some outreach projects execute parts of their work on the streets, quite literally reaching out, going to where the people are. One such example in London would be Streetwise, a project that works with young men who rent themselves. This project offers counselling, advice, information about safer sex, and practical help and support (Streetwise Youth, 1995). Lesbian and gay youth provision has also had a component of outreach, to maximise the number of individuals who may benefit from such provision. Burnham, writing in the American context, explores the possibility of community initiatives with lesbian and gay communities. He argues that social workers within social work agencies could play a role in facilitating lesbian and gay community initiatives:

> The social worker who delivers services directly may be in the most strategic position to offer members of oppressed populations (including lesbian women and gay men) encouragement, support, advocacy, consultation, and direction in organising to impact environmental systems. (Burnham, 1992: 145)

Whatever the form of intervention, the context or the organisation, a primary concern for social work should be how to make their services accessible to, welcoming and inclusive of all individuals and communities in need of them.

7

Children and Families

The parenting of children, how we parent and who should parent provokes powerful feelings.

The social and historical context

The family is the context in which the vast majority of people have been parented. It has also been a central building block in most societies and cultures. How the family should be constructed, and who its constituents can and should be, have been key areas of ideological debate (Barrett and McIntosh, 1982; Brosnan, 1996). The 'family' is often taken to mean a two-generational household, made up of a married heterosexual couple and their birth children, the nuclear family. This particular form of 'family' has had tremendous ideological meaning over and above a particular form of parental unit.

As outlined in Chapter 3, the question of who should parent and what can constitute 'the family' has been an integral part of an anti-lesbian and gay platform which has been acted out in debates over certain aspects of legislation in Britain over the last ten years. Over the same period there have been a plethora of publications relevant to social workers about lesbian and gay families and parenting (Hanscombe and Forster, 1982; Rights of Women Lesbian Custody Group, 1986; Boston Lesbian Psychologies Collective, 1987; Pollack and Vaughn, 1987; Bozett, 1989a; Bozett and Sussman, 1990; Rafkin, 1990; Woodman, 1992; Martin, 1993; Mason, 1994; Patterson, 1994; Arnup, 1995; Campion, 1995; Wakling and Bradstock, 1995; Ali, 1996; Saffron, 1996). The perceived threat of lesbian and gay households parenting children, to children, the family and society, has been a powerful force over a considerable period. The stage where much of this anxiety has been acted out has been the courts, in awarding custody to fathers in cases of parental separation, where the mother has been a lesbian (GLC, 1986; Radford and Cobley, 1987). Often these judgements have been made irrespective of the nature of the attachment between the child and its respective parents. The judges' summings-up have often indicated the ideological basis on which these judgements have been made. However, social workers have also been implicated in these decisions:

> The courts have often upheld popular prejudices about lesbian parenthood in their decisions to award custody to fathers on the grounds of the mother being a lesbian in disputed cases . . . Evidence from the Lesbian Custody Project shows that social workers have been instrumental in lesbian mothers losing their children, through recommendations in their social enquiry reports (Radford and Cobley, 1987). These social workers were guided by ignorance and prejudice, not by research, evidence and knowledge. These actions have grave implications for mothers, but most significantly for the children, whose interests the social workers are meant to be safeguarding. (Brown, 1992a: 214)

Over the last ten years there has been a considerable shift in the attitudes of the courts, the situation now being that a decision to award custody to the father solely on the basis of the mother's homosexuality would be the rarity not the rule. This change has happened for various reasons, a major one being the results of research both in Britain and in America, stimulated by lesbian custody cases, that contradicted 'common-sense' beliefs that children would be damaged if their parent was lesbian or gay.

The ideological debate has moved its focus from who should have custody of children in the cases of parental separation, where the primary focus was on lesbian mothering, to who should be allowed to foster and adopt, which has been relevant to lesbians and gay men alike. However, even though the attitudes of some judges, influenced by the arguments put forward from research, may have affected their judgements in custody cases, this research has had little influence on public attitudes:

> In most western countries, the last three decades has seen a gradual emergence into public life of those who are gay or lesbian. There has been increasing tolerance of people who openly wear

the badge of homosexuality, to the extent that most heterosexual people do not attempt to interfere as long as it does not encroach on their lives – that is to say, as long as gay people are discreet or keep their sexuality a private matter. However, any suggestion of openly gay or lesbian adults as parents seems to produce a huge outcry – somehow, having children brings parents into a public arena where their personal lives can be justifiably criticised. All the age-old arguments come flying forth: homosexuality is sinful, perverted, unnatural. (Campion, 1995: 177)

Although it is likely that lesbians and gay men have always fostered, it is the public acknowledgement of this that has appeared to be intolerable. For agencies to consciously choose to place children with lesbians and gay men, seemed a heresy. The debates that surrounded the fostering guidelines and the adoption White Paper (Chapter 3) bear witness to this. Whitfield, responding to this debate in 1991, wrote:

Bearing in mind all that we know about inter-generational transmission of psychosocial security, it is imperative that public policies affecting children genuinely reflect what we know from research, rather than the wishes of interest groups whose needs and contributions to society can actually be met in other ways. (Whitfield, 1991: 16)

This intervention into the fostering and adoption debate demonstrates the intimate connection between values and knowledge. Whitfield is calling on research to back his value-based position but at the same time, either deliberately or unwittingly, ignoring the relevant research in this area that challenges his assumptions. I have argued elsewhere that the public acknowledgement of lesbian and gay fostering and adoption and the actual increase in the numbers involved since the 1970s is to do with the increasing confidence of lesbians and gay men and changes in local government:

As local government has endeavoured to be more open, the public has made more demands that services should reflect the needs of a heterogeneous community. This process included lesbians and gay men becoming more vocal and more confident in taking opportunities to more fully participate in society. This included wanting to be able to offer the skills some individuals felt they had as carers, both for adults and for children. (Brown, 1991: 12)

Martin argues that there was another important factor, namely the profession's need to recruit a more diverse group of carers than had previously been the case. She writes:

Recognition of the ill-effects of the long-term care, children 'drifting in care', and a new focus on the need for security and permanence for all children led to a change in emphasis on adoption and fostering. Older children, sibling groups, black children, children with disabilities and children with emotional and behavioural difficulties started to be placed by a few pioneering agencies. This new range of children called for a change in recruitment of prospective parents. As one such agency, Parents for Children, puts it, they encouraged 'unusual parents for unusual children'. (Martin, 1993: 122)

Preventative work with and support to families

Against this backdrop and the increasing awareness and acceptance in many quarters of social work of the diversity of different family forms, some social work organisations began to address all areas of service delivery directed to families from agencies. This process was partly due to the pressure placed on social work departments by equality units (see Chapter 3) within their own organisations, the increase in the relevant research base, the employment of out lesbians and gay men within social work, and the gradual realisation that the numbers of families in touch with social work agencies where a lesbian was the primary carer had increased or become more visible or both.

The diversity of these particular families and the 'ordinariness' of their difficulties began to erode some social workers' tendency to stereotype lesbians and gay men.

Much of the assumptive world of social workers in relationship to lesbian and gay parenting had been constructions of stereotypes and 'common sense'. The research into this area of parenting has exploded many comfortable assumptions about such areas as the development of gender-identity and sexuality. It is beyond the possibility of this chapter to review the research literature in any detail here: excellent summaries that are accessible and cover research both in America and Britain already exist (Tasker and Golombok, 1991; Patterson, 1992; Campion, 1995; Tasker and Golombok, 1995). The main themes of the research can be identified as being: gender identity, sexuality, stigma, educational and emotional development, and peer relationships. This research was originally stimulated by lesbian custody cases, covered in the previous section. Because of this, its original focus was on comparisons between children growing up in heterosexual and homosexual households where the child remained with the mother after a separation from the father. This research was complicated methodologically as these children had been exposed to parental separation that may well have been more critical to their development than the sexual-orientation of their parents. The bulk of the research has been focused on lesbian mothers rather than gay fathers. More recently, with the realisation that many lesbian mothers choose to have children as lesbians, and may never have lived with the child's father, there has been a research interest focusing on the development of the children within these households (Patterson, 1994; Tasker and Golombok, 1995).

A brief summary of some of the key findings from the research would include the following.

Studies looking at gender identity showed no significant differences between children growing up in lesbian or gay households and those within heterosexual ones (Green, 1978; Kirkpatrick *et al.*, 1981; Golombok *et al.*, 1983; Green *et al.*, 1986).

Research into gender role behaviour concludes no significant difference between children of heterosexual and homosexual households (Green, 1978; Hoeffer, 1981; Kirkpatrick *et al.*, 1981; Golombok *et al.*, 1983; Green *et al.*, 1986; Gottman, 1990).

The question of the development of sexual orientation has provoked much controversy. The research findings contradict assumptions that heterosexuality can only be guaranteed by living with heterosexual parents (the overwhelming majority of lesbians and gay men grew up in such families). Research findings show no difference between the sexual identity formation between the children of homosexual and heterosexual households (Green, 1978; Miller, 1979; Golombok *et al.*, 1983; Huggins, 1989; Gottman,

1990). Studies looking at this specifically in relation to gay fathers showed the same results (Bozett, 1982, 1987, 1989b).

Patterson summarises the findings:

> Overall, then, development of gender identity, gender role behaviour, and sexual preference among offspring of gay and lesbian parents was found to fall within normal bounds. (Patterson, 1992: 1031)

Other areas of comparison have been studied, including comparative rates of psychiatric disturbance (Kirkpatrick *et al.*, 1981; Golombok, 1983); behavioural and emotional difficulties (Golombok, 1983); personality characteristics (Gottman, 1990); self-concept (Huggins, 1989); intelligence (Green *et al.*, 1986). There were no significant differences indicated between the children of the different groups studied in any of these findings (Patterson, 1992).

A major area of concern for social workers around lesbian and gay parenting has focused on children's social relationships. Social work focuses on the individual in their social context and this was an obvious, relevant and legitimate area of concern. Patterson (1992) reviews the research covering this area. In relation to peer relationships (Green, 1978; Golombok *et al.*, 1983) and popularity (Green *et al.*, 1986), there were no significant differences. Lesbians were found to be more concerned than heterosexual women that their children had positive contact with adult men (Kirkpatrick, 1981). This theme was supported by the findings of Golombok *et al.*, (1983), which showed that children of lesbians had more frequent contact with their fathers after the parental separation than did children of heterosexual mothers. Stigmatisation has also been shown not to be a particular problem for children of lesbian and gay households (Green, 1978; Green *et al.*, 1986).

Another area of concern has been the belief that homosexual men and women are more likely to sexually abuse children. The research completely contradicts that assumption (Groth and Birnbaum, 1978; Sarafino, 1979; Jones and MacFarlane, 1980; Finkelhor and Russell, 1984).

In summary the research to date shows no significant differences for children growing up in heterosexual or homosexual households in terms of risk or of their overall psychosexual, intellectual and social development. Preventative work with families must start from the position of an awareness of this knowledge base, as otherwise many inaccurate assumptions can be made, leading to inappropriate interventions.

Little has been written (Brown, 1992a; Gunter, 1992; Martin, 1993) about preventative social work with lesbian and gay families. This section therefore draws on other relevant literature and my own practice, both as a local authority social work manager in a London borough and in my experience as a consultant to social work organisations. The lack of a significant literature is marked, both within the social work and lesbian and gay arenas. The former can be explained by a lack of awareness of the numbers of lesbian and gay parents that are in contact with social work agencies, partly owing to their 'invisibility', since a significant quantity of these parents never come out. The latter is more complex. Lesbians and gay men have for many years been struggling for the right to parent. This inevitably leads to the emphasis being placed on the right to parent and the strengths of lesbians and gay men as parents. However, lesbians and gay men are not a homogeneous group, and individuals may need social work intervention and service provision for all the same reasons that heterosexual parents may need them. Like heterosexuals, they will have relationship break-downs, bereavements, issues around disabilities, domestic violence, emotional difficulties, coping with poverty, difficulties with family dynamics, in other words the ordinary things that many people have to cope with or have to seek assistance in relation to. However, as an oppressed group, there has been a tendency not to want to wash the dirty linen in public for fear that everyday upset, or more fundamental crisis, difficulties or real disturbance will be attributed solely to sexual-orientation, that the stereotypes will take precedence over the specific, unique individual in their own context. This shying away from the admission that 'sometimes things really do go wrong', however understandable, perpetuates oppression because it contributes to lesbian and gay individuals and families not receiving the support they may need. It also contributes to the tendency of social work organisations to avoid having to seriously consider the quality and appropriateness of their service delivery to lesbians and gay men.

Some social work organisations have considered their services to lesbian and gay families. One such organisation, a London local authority social services department, reviewed their services in this light while creating a new childcare policy in preparation for the introduction of the Children Act, 1989. This process included my employment both as a consultant to the process and as author of an advisory document. The document stated:

> The Social Services Department notes that good social work practice will mean that the focus of work with lesbian and gay clients will address their total experience and work with each person's unique individuality, and that their sexual orientation will not be seen as the dominant aspect that the Social Services Department should address. (Brown, 1990: 2)

Gunter has a positive view of the potentialities in this area:

> Social work as a profession is in a unique position to address the many and varied problems encountered by gay men and lesbian women within the conceptual framework of family. The dual perspective of social work, focusing on both the individual and the social environment, provides a foundation for effective interventions with gay and lesbian people. (Gunter, 1992: 87)

The provision of a competent service to families, in addition to considerations of good practice generally, will mean developing a commitment to working in partnership and in ways that are empowering. The following considerations have to be taken on board.

> Social work agencies must take cognisance of organisational matters that affect lesbians and gay men accessing services outlined in Chapter 6.
>
> Social work managers need to consider supervision of this work as outlined in Chapter 6.
>
> Social workers need to take into account that, even where they and their agency are welcoming of lesbians and gay men and where there would not be an inappropriate focus on sexuality if it were irrelevant to the matter in hand, the service user/client may have a very different perception. There must be a strong focus on the skills of engagement on the part of the social worker to enable sufficient trust to be established for effective work to be undertaken.

Child protection

People abuse their children for a whole range of highly complex reasons and there is a huge body of literature which debates the many different arguments addressing the question of 'why'. Although there is scant material that specifically addresses lesbian and gay parents who abuse their children, there is little reason to assume that lesbians and gay men are not subject to the same degree of complexity in relation to causation. This is an area where there is even less literature than with the previous section, and where it is not just that the 'ordinary has gone wrong', but it is where parents actively harm their children. For obvious reasons, in the present political climate, this is an area that lesbians and gay men may not wish to dwell on and certainly not one they wish to air in public. I draw here on my own professional involvement and experience with five child protection cases involving lesbian mothers. I have no equivalent experience with gay men as parents. The nature of the abuse towards the children covered the whole range of neglect, emotional, physical and sexual abuse.

The families were diverse: single-parents, Black women, white women and couples co-parenting. The reasons why these women (eight in total) had come to the situation of abusing or neglecting their children were the same complex reasons why individuals might generally be vulnerable to abusing their children. For example, one mother was unable to form an attachment to her daughter, partly because of her own early rejection by her own parents. In none of the cases was the sexual-orientation of these women a factor affecting the decisions for there to be statutory intervention. However, there was an awareness that there may have been factors over and above general 'vulnerability factors' that may have contributed to these adults abusing their children which needed to be borne in mind. These were primarily in relation to the complex impacts of oppression on individuals:

> When we are working with lesbians who abuse their children, we need to have some general understanding of the pressures on women and the additional pressures on lesbians that may lead them to such behaviour (Brown, 1986; Parton and Parton, 1988). (Brown, 1992a: 214)

There were other significant themes that emerged from this tiny sample of child protection cases. The women involved all, initially, had additional anxieties about state intervention over and above those expressed by most working-class and Black women. They assumed their parenting would be scrutinised in relation to their sexual-orientation and nothing else.

The assumption that is sometimes voiced in anti-discriminatory practice literature, that if the social worker is from the same oppressed group as the service user/client, then the quality of service provision is improved, was not borne out in this small sample:

> Even in this tiny sample of cases there was a variety of social workers involved, in terms of gender, race and sexual orientation. The quality of work done was dictated by the competence of the social work input, and the workers' ability to form appropriate, skilled relationships with the clients. The intervention outcomes were not affected by the sexual orientation of the workers, but by their abilities. (Brown, 1992a: 215)

This may also have been a reflection of the importance of the values and ethos of the particular organisation and its commitment to the supervision of staff.

The work with these families illuminated a 'culture' gap at that time, between the discourses of the predominantly working-class lesbians involved and the agencies' adoption of predominantly middle-class lesbian and gay 'professional-speak'. Social workers used the term lesbian; the women predominantly referred to themselves as gay. Professional terms such as 'co-parenting' for two women sharing the care of children was experienced as an unfamiliar language. One couple used the terms 'mum' and 'dad' to delineate the roles they had taken on within the family. As can be imagined, this use of terminology generated a little professional anxiety. Their use of 'mum' and 'dad', when explored, was their attempt at being accepted in a homophobic world, rather than any gender confusion: 'We should not assume a common language, or interpret others' use of words on face value' (Brown, 1992a: 215).

Child protection work necessitates close multi-professional working. In any one of these cases there was the mobilisation of a variety of state agencies: police, health, education, the NSPCC, and the social services department. The experiences varied when liaising with these agencies, 'ranging from sensitive clear non-discriminatory input, through liberal stereotyping of the most unhelpful nature, to outright homophobia' (Brown, 1992a: 215).

The positive stereotyping (wishing only to see the positives irrespective of the reality) deserves to be addressed separately. This has already been referred to earlier. In this context it was evident in one situation:

> Positive stereotyping happened in one of our cases, where the commitment to lesbian parenting, for a short time, predominated over the interests of the child. This mother's activities were seen in a prejudiced and distorted way: 'I thought that was normal for lesbians.' Any stereotyping, where people see a particular individual as a type, will not be in anyone's interest, particularly children's. (Brown, 1992a: 216)

The consultation process with the London local authority culminated with some simple recommendations, which I will quote in full, in conclusion. Although it refers to a particular agency, these suggestions are relevant to all social work organisations involved in preventative work and child protection:

> staff . . . may hold overt or covert prejudiced attitudes and be ignorant in respect of lesbian and gay parenting; this will need to be dealt with through training and supervision as this group of workers will be expected to be able to make informed assessments in relation to good parenting.
>
> All Team Leaders have a key role in relation to child protection in respect of supervision . . . There has to be a trusting, open, supervisory relationship to facilitate learning, confrontation, exploration and accountability within child protection work. This is particularly pertinent in this area where workers may feel hesitant, de-skilled and frightened to make judgements that may be necessary. (Brown, 1990: 8)

The recommendations continue, addressing the problem of stereotyping:

> There is a great danger that this may also be applicable to lesbian and gay families where their sexual orientation may be seen as the

primary focus, so that their unique emotional life experiences, which will affect their own subjective experiences of homosexuality, and society's reaction to it, are ignored.

Each family has to be worked with in its total complexity, not with superficial stereotyped assumptions, whether these be positive or negative.

Social workers have to walk a tightrope between the protection of the child within a family, and establishing a good working relationship with the adult, when working within the child protection field.

Childcare Enquiries repeatedly indicate we are sometimes better at forming relationships with adults than protecting the children. This may be exacerbated when the worker understands the additional pressures and difficulties some lesbian and gay parents may experience, living in a homophobic society. The interests of the child are paramount, however understandable the adult's predicament, and this should constantly be reinforced in the supervisory process. The key points in the section include:

(i)   the necessity as a worker to be aware of his or her own ignorance and prejudice, to enable them to work more effectively;
(ii)   the necessity to see each family and individual in their total complexity, not to fall back on superficial stereotypes;
(iii) to always focus on the child in any situation;
(iv) for social workers to receive adequate supervision to facilitate the above. (Brown, 1990: 8–10)

Fostering and adoption

Much of the hostility to lesbians and gay men fostering and adopting has been backed by 'common-sense' attitudes about children being unable to develop 'normally' within lesbian and gay households, although the research evidence covered earlier in this chapter would refute those opinions. Both the need of the social work profession to diversify its recruitment of carers and the British government's interventions in this area have been covered earlier. This section focuses on the assessment of lesbians and gay men as potential carers, and support to those carers when they have been approved.

There is still a lack of uniformity between different childcare agencies about whether or not they welcome lesbian and gay applicants. Martin sees adoption and fostering by lesbians and gay men as being more accepted in America than in Britain. Referring to America, she writes:

> Many social workers [who] wouldn't have dreamed of placing a child in a gay family ten years ago now do so without hesitation. More agencies are willing to facilitate adoptions to openly gay applicants. (Martin, 1993: 125)

Bozett takes a slightly different view, arguing that in some parts of America the use of lesbian and gay foster carers would not be considered and, where they are, there are similar trends to those that have been identified in Britain:

> . . . homosexual applicants are scrutinised more carefully and are held to a higher standard than are their heterosexual counterparts . . . in addition prospective homosexual foster or adoptive parents may find that only difficult-to-place children are made available to them . . . (Bozett and Sussman, 1990: 104)

The recruitment and assessment of lesbian and gay prospective carers in the British context has been covered more fully elsewhere (Skeates and Jabri, 1988; Brown, 1991; Hicks, 1996). The most important objective in the area of fostering and adoption has to be the recruitment of the best possible people as carers: people who will be able to form caring, containing, facilitative, understanding and productive relationships with children and young people. The attributes that contribute to a person's ability to do this are not dependent on their sexual orientation.

In just the same way that lesbians and gay men who have to be in contact with social work organisations may assume a hostility towards them, this is also the case with lesbian and gay applicants. To approach an assessment of a lesbian or gay applicant requires that the social worker be familiar with the relevant knowledge base, consider their own and their agency's values in relation to lesbians and gay men as parents, and have the appropriate skills to under-take a full assessment. Hicks's work, which looks at lesbians' and gay applicants' experiences of the assessment process, would suggest that social workers are not always prepared in the ways suggested above, but rather the reverse (Hicks, 1996). Social workers have found themselves in the invidious position of directly experiencing some of the contradictory processes that have been prevalent since 1979. Central government has articulated hostility to lesbian and gay fostering and adoption, which it has acted out through various interventions in the drawing up of related legislation, at the same time as some local governments have been developing more positive policies towards the recruitment of lesbians and gay men. In Chapter 2, four levels of values were outlined that need to be considered in relation to every piece of social work (p. 20). These were: first, the values of the service user/client in relation to a particular piece of work; second, the values of the social worker in relation to the same work; third, the values of the agency in relation to the work; and, last, the values enshrined in the policies and legislative context in which the piece of work is being undertaken. In undertaking an assessment of lesbian or gay prospective carers, it is easy to see how a number of these levels may be in conflict. This is an area where social workers need supervisory support, in managing these conflicts when they occur.

There remains a debate in social work practice about whether assessments should be the same, irrespective of the applicant's sexual-orientation, or whether there should be additional areas covered in assessments of lesbians and gay men, because of the oppression they face and the possible internalisation and identification with it. This argument is controversial because the 'additional areas' have, in the past, often reflected the agencies' ignorance of relevant research (covered earlier), or their preoccupation with oppressive assumptions, often reflected in an over-emphasis on behalf of the worker with homosexual sex. As with child protection assessments, assessments of prospective lesbian and gay prospective carers should build on the strengths of competent fostering and adoption practice and, in addition, consider the following.

When the discourses surrounding an oppressed group indicate a specific assumption, that assumption should be critically analysed. An example would be stigma. One of the main planks in the argument against the use of lesbians and gay men as substitute carers has been that it would not be fair to place vulnerable children with stigmatised adults. However, the actual situation may be quite the reverse. Lesbians and gay men who have learnt how to survive and manage stigma may have developed a number of strengths through this process. Children in need of placements are a stigmatised group. In care or been in care are terms that carry social meaning well beyond the simple transfer of information:

> Coping with stigma is often a strengthening, enriching process, as well as a harrowing one. We need to be recruiting people who have developed through their experiences, and not those who have been crushed by them. (Brown, 1991: 16)

Assessments need to examine how individuals have negotiated the management of stigma. In addition the assessment process should address:

1. The individual's experience of their homosexuality, their own and their family's response historically.
2. How confident they feel in relation to their sexual orientation, how comfortable they are as lesbians and gay men.
3. How homophobia and heterosexism have impinged on their lives, and how they feel they've dealt with this, and what present coping devices they now use.
4. What are their present relationships – sexual, emotional, supportive, family, etc.? How do they negotiate homophobia within close relationships, e.g. siblings?
5. With reference to the future, how they have thought about relating to birth parents of foster children, how they have thought about relationships with outside carers e.g. schools, play groups, child minders . . .?
(Brown, 1991: 16)

Reticence about approaching these areas is often on the behalf of the assessor. Lesbians and gay men have usually spent much time thinking about these areas, and discussing them with a social worker, in a non-oppressive way, need not be threatening.

One key area that this raises is the question of the assessment of heterosexual applicants. I have argued elsewhere that sex and sexuality are areas that should be integral to every assessment:

> the subjects of gender, sex and sexuality need to be firmly and permanently placed within the assessment process. These are areas of human emotion and activity that have direct implications

for children we place with carers: and we have a responsibility to ensure that the carers with whom we are working have the ability to offer a comfortable framework in which children and young people can develop. (Brown, 1992b: 30)

Many agencies have assessed lesbians and gay men as suitable foster and adoptive parents, but fewer have in practice placed children with them, or, where they have, there has been a tendency to place children who are referred to as 'hard to place'. This could be that they are seen as somehow second best. This says as much about agencies' attitudes towards children who are 'hard to place' as it does about their attitudes towards lesbian and gay carers. The moves towards working in partnership with birth parents, and openness with them about the carers being considered, are often cited as problematic areas when considering the use of a lesbian or gay carer. This may reflect the ambivalence of the social worker. When they are confident that a placement with a particular person or couple is the best one for a specific child, and are able to articulate their reasons, then they are more likely to be able to convey this to a birth parent. There also seems to be an underlying assumption in these arguments that all birth parents are homophobic. Birth parents have differing responses, and there are instances of them choosing homosexual carers (Sage, 1991).

Support and training are contributions agencies have a responsibility to offer to carers while they are waiting for placements and after they are being used. Sex and sexuality need to be integral to training, and there are excellent examples of the inclusion of this material in general training packages that now exist (National Foster Care Association, 1994).

Over and above support that should come to carers directly from the social work agency, lesbians and gay men need to be made aware of organisations like the Lesbian and Gay Foster and Adoption Parent Network, which acts as a network and information exchange in Britain.

Young people

For a significant number of lesbians and gay men, the realisation that they are homosexual happens in their adolescence. Taking

Erikson's (1965) life cycle approach, this is the time where the fifth stage of the life cycle, 'identity versus confusion', is being negotiated. Gibson writes:

> If one considers the fundamental importance of a sense of identity to the individual personality, of being a specific person within an understood environment, one gets an impression of the potential depth of conflict inherent in this life crisis. (Gibson, 1991: 43)

For young lesbians and gay men there may be additional conflicts associated with this process. Coming out or being found out often provokes an initial crisis in families. The very foundation of security for the majority of young lesbians and gay men up to that time can suddenly seem fairly insecure. At adolescence, to be propelled into the realities of surviving in a homophobic world can be traumatic. Young lesbians and gay men rarely have role models of adult lesbians and gay men in their lives and as a result there is often little support and a strong possibility of the young person internalising or identifying with oppressive views of homosexuality and, as a consequence, negative feelings about themselves (Robertson, 1981; Suriyaprakasam, 1995). All these factors may be particularly intense for young people 'in care'.

In the British context, the thinking about the position of young lesbians and gay men has been initiated from within the youth service provision (Trenchard and Warren, 1985). There has been dialogue within the service about how well equipped youth workers are in relating positively to this area (Kent-Baguley, 1985, 1990; Heathfield, 1988). One of the most important publications to come out of this was *Something To Tell You* (Trenchard and Warren, 1984), the report of the findings of a research project undertaken by the London Gay Teenage Group in 1983. The research examined, by the use of questionnaires, 416 young people's experience of family, school, the Youth Service, employment, coming out, going out and making friends, sex and relationships, pressures, problems and the police. The research illustrated the individual and collective strengths of young lesbians and gay men, but it also showed the insufferable additional pressures these young people are subjected to as a result of societal attitudes towards homosexuality. One of the most disturbing findings of this research was that 19 per cent of the respondents had attempted suicide, evenly distributed in relation to gender:

The cumulative effects of a negative self-image, problems at school, the experience of isolation, a lack of the usual support networks, family rejection and so on can lead to a young person feeling quite helpless. One young man at a discussion group told us: 'I really did think that I was the only young gay. That's what made me take the tablets, attempt suicide.' (Trenchard and Warren, 1984: 145)

The youth service provision is an example of where the mainstream service has allowed (in some areas and after considerable struggles) for the autonomous provision of lesbian and gay groups within itself.

Social workers are sometimes involved in the crisis point where a young person's homosexuality has been revealed to their family. Lovell vividly describes the dilemmas and dynamics involved in this process for families as well as offering constructive interventions and resolutions (Lovell, 1995). Crisis intervention theory and its application is particularly relevant here, whether this is their birth, adoptive or foster family. O'Hagan's useful book (1986) is particularly relevant, because these interventions are often conflictual and sometimes involve statutory intervention. The initial feelings of shock and rejection can be worked with in most cases, to facilitate the re-emergence of the more important feelings of attachment that will enable the family to adjust to this new aspect of the young person's identity:

Family members undergoing this redefinition and development of new values and roles need factual, unbiased information about homosexuality to help them gain a balanced perspective on the trauma they are experiencing . . . By providing facilitating, non-pejorative assistance to the family, we can lessen the confusion and uncertainty these families experience as they wrestle with the reconstruction of long-held but never-examined beliefs and assumptions, and help them to keep the intimate circle of the family intact and healthy. (Strommen, 1990: 29)

For some young people, although only a small proportion, this is never achieved and can result in homelessness, with all the risks attached or of being accommodated, going into care. Agencies like the Albert Kennedy Trust (see Chapter 6) play a crucial part in trying to prevent and/or alleviate some of the potential damage to young people that may result from these circumstances. The Children Act 1989's guidance states that the needs and concerns of gay men and lesbian women must also be recognised and approached sympathetically (Department of Health, 1991c: 97). There is an increasing awareness of these needs and concerns, in the British context, as the result of the impact of the Albert Kennedy Trust and the autonomous organisation of young lesbians and gay men within the National Association of Young People in Care. All young people, homosexual or heterosexual, need information about safer sex that is accessible, explicit and clear, and to have it conveyed to them in a way that is relevant both to sex in all its wider meanings, and to the specific life experiences of each individual young person. The responsibility for this lies with the adults to whom the well-being of the young people concerned is entrusted.

Every aspect of childcare practice and work with families needs to be reviewed to examine whether we do have the knowledge, values and skills to offer an appropriate intervention to lesbians and gay men and those close to them, to enable the best possible outcomes for those involved.

8

Social Work with Adults

This chapter covers material relevant for social workers working with lesbians and gay men as adults in their own right, separate from their capacity as carers of children or as offenders. They may, as adults, indeed be carers of children and/or offenders, but here this is not the primary focus. Because in this context the term 'adult' is so broad, I have had to be selective in what is covered. There are generic themes that are relevant to all interventions with adults, but in addition there are areas that are particularly relevant to lesbian and gay clients/service users, including mental health, chronic sickness, death and bereavement, physical disability, old age, and learning disabilities (those headings not covered include substance misuse (except briefly under mental health in relation to alcohol) and the assessment of adult carers who are lesbians and gay men). With so much to deal with in one chapter, the intention is to offer pointers or to raise questions for further thought, rather than engage in exhaustive discussions.

Generic themes

Social work with adults is primarily focused on the assessment of need or risk and on the provision of services that might meet the need or alleviate the risk. The alleviation of risk might involve statutory intervention against an individual's wishes. The statutes that dictate the nature of assessment, definitions of need and ideas as to what constitutes risk will be dependent on the national and organisational context in which the social worker is located. In addition the organisational variety in work with adults is considerable, both within the sectors whose primary function might be assessment and care management and also in the provider sector, although in practice there is often an overlap.

Assessment was covered in Chapter 6. The view is taken in this chapter that the most effective model of assessment in working with adults is the exchange model, described by Smale *et al.* (1993). This is the model most likely to promote participation, empowerment and partnership, and the least likely to be oppressive and discriminatory, because, by definition, the social worker has to work with the individuals and systems involved within their own context, and has to 'hear' what is actually being said, which is often not what we might expect to hear. What I refer to as 'the individual in their own context', which Coulshed refers to as 'people in relation to their environment' (1991: 24), has to include the social and political context in which these individuals exist. So, for example, referring a gay man to a day centre which has never considered its service provision to lesbians and gay men and where staff participate in homophobic dialogue and jokes, is unlikely to engender feelings of respect, welcome or inclusion. Lesbians and gay men are subject to oppressive ideas, emotions and behaviours from others. How these are perceived and experienced will be unique to the individual, and although there will often be perceptions and experiences in common with others, as social workers we can never assume that commonality. The assumption of a common experience for oppressed groups has been one of the most oppressive aspects of social work, as damaging in its consequences as being ignorant of or ignoring the oppression that might impact on individuals and communities.

Social work with adults is where the final aspect of discrimination covered in Chapter 6, the 'interrelationship of different structural oppressions', is acutely visible. The headings covered earlier – mental health, chronic sickness, physical disability, old age and learning disabilities – are all constructed categories, which attract oppressive ideas and behaviours in their own right. To have any of the above relevant to you is to be marginalised, made peripheral, patronised, pitied, talked about or for but not with, ridiculed, made less than human. Like homosexuality they also provoke embarrassment, and become the prism through which a person is perceived by others. The person's unique, complex individuality is something that becomes tacked on to the all-consuming label; 'the woman in the bed with breast cancer'. This interrelationship of structural oppressions has often been referred to as a double burden or double oppression. Stuart criticises the use of this term in relation to Black disabled people, arguing that it may be inadequate: 'the phrase "double oppression" is rather empty; rhetoric has replaced clear thinking' (1993: 93). Morris makes similar criticisms of what she refers to as 'the "double disadvantage" trap' (1993: 89), which she considers in relation to gender and disability. People who are subject to two or more oppressive social and political realities do not experience them as independent entities but as complexly interrelated in their impact on the unique individual concerned. This means, for example, that disablement and homophobia are not necessarily experienced separately but may come together in quite unique ways. It also means that a disabled gay man cannot necessarily rely on separate ways of combating disablement and homophobia but may have to look for new ways to manage the impacts of the interrelationship of the two. The experience of the interrelationships of oppressions is often seen as a 'double burden', a terrible, negative thing, a reinforcement of a victim ideology. I would wish to challenge this perception. It may be that the experience of oppression as well as being debilitating can also be a source of the development of new perceptions, feelings, strengths and skills and that the development of these abilities in relation to one source of oppression may be transferable to another.

The whole question of 'need' and the 'assessment of need' is a subject that has attracted considerable attention (Oliver and Barnes, 1993). The very terms themselves assume a dependence on others to prescribe what a need is, and how it would best be met. Needs thus defined are quite different from rights. The term 'needs' is often used in the sense of basic common denominators, with an underlying assumption of passivity on the behalf of the recipient. That is, 'needs' often mean only the fundamental minima of basic personal care, mobility, access, emotional stability, which are quite different from what is desired and wished for, including pleasure and high quality. I might need to be fed, and I will need good nutritional food to sustain my health, but I might also desire to have certain kinds of food to be prepared in certain kinds of ways, not just because it meets, for example, my 'cultural needs' but because I want it. Desire and the fulfilment of wishes and wants, even when they are not realised, are crucial aspects of human experience, fantasy and psychological well-being. To reduce these for particular groups of individuals, to subsume them under needs and then to have them defined by others, is potentially dehumanising.

Under current social conditions and in the social and political contexts within which social work operates, it is outside both the brief and possibility to satisfy all the desires that individuals may express. However, it is the denial of this lack that is often dehumanising. One of the contradictory phenomena over the last decade has arisen out of the onset of HIV and AIDS. Many of the non-statutory services that have developed within the provider sectors have addressed what people want, as well as what they need. The facilities and services provided by some agencies range well beyond most concepts of basic personal care, mobility, access and emotional stability. Out of devastation and despair have come varied, quality resources offering choice and the possibility to meet some desires as well as needs. One hopes that the stark contrast between some of what is provided here, and what is provided by mainstream care will raise the question of comparative quality, for example, the boring tedium that many older people are subjected to in some residential establishments with no choice of having the television on or off, let alone of programme to watch. For social workers to acknowledge the limitations of what they can supply is more facilitative than if they do not. It also validates the whole person rather than operating as if that person was just a bundle of unfeeling, undesiring needs.

Independence has become fetishised in social work practice and discourses. Social work has developed a compulsive-obsessive relationship to it. Independence is often a goal that many clients/service users are encouraged to move towards or have imposed upon them. This has been excellently described in relation to physical disability (French, 1993), but can also be applied to other areas of dependency, for example the psychological dependency on an employed carer of someone suffering from depression. Many people do want independence, but there is confusion about what it means. Independence is a different thing from autonomy and control. What is often lacking is not independence but a person having control over their dependency. Most people are dependent in some way both materially and emotionally, and that is seen as desirable. Most intimate, sexual partnerships have a component of mutual dependency, which is not frowned upon. There is a tendency in relation to specific groups to equate dependency with weakness. Many adults who have social work involvement will need to be dependent in some way. Individuals may need to be facilitated to feel more control in how they negotiate dependency and not to feel negative or patronised by it. The responsibility for this lies with the commitment to partner-ship and negotiation, between the carer, provider or social worker and the individuals concerned. This process of negotiation may be problematic for lesbians and gay men who may feel vulnerable, especially where they feel their sexuality has to be hidden. For example, if I am a woman paralysed after a stroke from the neck down, how can I ask my home carer, employed to facilitate my 'independent living', to switch on Dyke TV (Channel 4, 1995) when I do not wish to reveal my sexual-orientation because the carer has already let me know their opinion that Beth Jordache's death on Brookside (Channel 4, 1995) was better than she deserved, because she was a lesbian!

Mental health and ill health

Lesbians and gay men are in the peculiar position of finding themselves subject to being categorised as mentally disordered even when they are feeling fine. The ninth revision of the World Health Organisation glossary and classification of mental disorder includes homosexuality under the subheading of sexual deviations and dis-orders, where it is listed along with bestiality (World Health Organisation, 1978). Although this was published nearly twenty years ago, it is relevant to how the mental health of lesbians and gay men is perceived, both by themselves and others. In Britain, the Mental Health Act 1983 made clear that 'sexual deviancy' alone could not constitute a mental disorder as defined within that Act (Jones, 1994). However, old beliefs and assumptions die hard, and it is necessary to separate the sexual-orientation of a person from their mental illness, as well as accepting that there may be an interrela-tionship for some people, in the sense that external homophobia and the possible internalisation of or identification with homophobia (Margolies *et al.*, 1987; Shildo, 1994) may become an additional 'vulnerability factor' for some people. Ashurst and Hall, state:

Lesbian women in distress seek understanding of the meaning of their distress, which will be as varied and as uniquely personal as that of any other individual. It should never be assumed that the distress is an inevitable consequence of lesbianism. (Ashurst and Hall, 1989: 95)

Lesbians and gay men who are labelled as mentally ill are likely to feel marginalised by the lesbian and gay communities and within the provisions that are there to offer help. Black lesbians and gay men within the mental health system may feel this even more acutely (Montsho, 1995). Marginalisation can increase feelings of alienation, something that is often present for people who are distressed or disturbed. 'People who are deemed to be mentally disordered often encounter a negative response, even to the point of outright hostility, from the community at large' (Thompson, 1993: 142) – the same can be said for lesbians and gay men. There is very little written about lesbians and gay men and mental illness, and there is a noticeable lack of such writing within the lesbian and gay texts that might address the issue. There is some material that covers related areas in looking at suicide (Rofes, 1990), and also a valuable recent paper on the experiences of Black lesbians and mental health (Montsho, 1995), but on the whole there does seem to be a real shying-away from this area, similar to that observed within the area of child abuse.

Lesbians and gay men go mad: to deny this would be oppressive. They go mad for the same complex reasons as heterosexuals do. They are not mad because they are homosexual. They need the same complex assessments and sensitive service delivery as anyone else. They may perceive that others associate their mental distress or disturbance with their sexual-orientation. In the British context, the Code of Practice for the Mental Health Act 1983 notes two important points in relation to assessments for possible admission to hospital for those who are suffering from a mental disorder:

> In judging whether compulsory admission is appropriate, those concerned should consider not only the statutory criteria but also . . . the risk of making assumptions based on a person's sex, social and cultural background or ethnic origin. (Department of Health, 1993b: 4)

This would seem particularly pertinent to lesbians and gay men, a group subject to much stereotyping and prejudice. The Code of Practice continues under the same general heading of assessment, that the Approved Social Worker needs to take into account 'the possibility of misunderstandings resulting from assumptions based on a person's sex, social and cultural background or ethnic origin' (Department of Health, 1993b: 6). Assessments are not just in relation to the possibility of compulsory admission to hospital, but will be primarily to do with accessing services and provision within the community. The Code of Practice's directives are just as relevant here.

Substance misuse is not a mental disorder, and by locating brief comments about it here I am not wishing to suggest that it is. However, it is sometimes exacerbated by emotional tension and distress and sometimes causes emotional tension and distress. Kus, in the context of America, describes alcohol misuse among lesbians and gay men as follows: 'One of the greatest problems facing adult gay and lesbian Americans [is] alcoholism and related forms of chemical dependencies' (1990b: 66). Kus, like many others, adopts a 'disease model' of alcohol misuse, and it is worth noting that many lesbians and gay men seem to be attracted to this set of ideas, both in relation to an explanation of alcohol misuse and also in relation to treatment. Alcoholics Anonymous has been used considerably by lesbians and gay men, to the extent that certainly in London, Sydney and San Francisco, and probably other cities, there is separate provision for lesbians and gay men.

There have been various explanations for the high rate of alcohol misuse (Ziebold and Mongeon, 1985; Nicoloff and Stiglitz, 1987; Kus, 1990c; Gonsiorek and Weinreich, 1991), including the gay bar theory, which states that because gay social culture is very concentrated in bars, lesbians and gay men are inevitably more vulnerable to alcohol misuse. Internalisation of or identification with homophobia is given as another contributory factor. This is the idea that such internalisation or identification can lead to low self-esteem and even to self-hatred, which in turn may contribute to misuse of alcohol. The crossing of traditional boundaries associated with gender roles has been cited as another factor, particularly for lesbians. This is relevant to the initiation of social or sexual contact, something that is associated with the bar culture. Women are socialised not to initiate contact, and although a lesbian may feel all right about being in the role of the initiator, it may stimulate quite high levels of tension that are alleviated by the use of alcohol.

Whatever the cause, alcohol is a serious health issue for lesbians and gay men. Alcohol services need to be sensitive to lesbians and gay men and to welcome them. Alcoholics Anonymous may be so popular because it has responded to lesbians and gay men in a positive way.

Chronic sickness, death and bereavement

These are not just problematic subjects for lesbians and gay men. Western cultures in recent history have developed processes of distancing and denial in relation to death and bereavement. They have been removed from the realms of the ordinary to exclusive practices, separating the dying away from their communities through the increased use of hospitalisation. The hospice movement has had a profound revolutionary impact on the accepted belief that the dying should be segregated and that death and dying should be taboo subjects. This challenging of the discourses of death and dying predated the onset of AIDS (Catalano, 1990). HIV and AIDS have forced public attention to matters of chronic sickness, death and dying in a way that even cancer had not. HIV and AIDS has had a disproportionate impact on gay men, particularly young ones and their friends, lovers and families (Edwards, 1992; Watney, 1994). This has meant devastation and loss for individuals and has had a profound impact on gay male communities and cultures. King reflects on the impact on the male gay community. He also notes the wider impact:

> It has long been apparent that few in the gay community were unaffected by the epidemic, even if they were not themselves HIV-positive. It soon became apparent as well that many outside the gay community were also deeply affected. There was clearly a ripple effect: for every person carrying the virus, there was a universe of loved ones who were affected. (King, 1995: 7)

Because of the seeming suddenness of the virus's onset, its devastating consequences, and its initial association with gay men, 'public perceptions of HIV during the last decade were distorted by misinformation, prejudice and difficulty in establishing the facts' (CCETSW, 1992: 6). The association of this virus with gayness did much to fuel homophobia. However, there have been some beneficial and unforeseen consequences of the onset of AIDS, difficult though this may be to accept. Such benefits include the bringing together of lesbians and gay men in response to both the virus and its consequences, but also to fight homophobia. Although lesbians are figured significantly low in the statistics as being affected by HIV or AIDS (O'Sullivan and Parmer, 1992), the antihomosexual fervour that was encouraged by the media would not have made the distinction between lesbians and gay men. Provisions and services which have been developed (predominantly by gay men) to care for people who are HIV-positive and who have AIDS have become models for others of how organisations can provide a high-quality service offering a degree of choice. Lastly, the onset of AIDS and HIV is assumed to have fuelled homophobia among 'the public'. However, 'the public' is made up of individuals and for some of them the experience may have been quite the reverse. Many employed carers were exposed to training around HIV and AIDS and, possibly for the first time, met lesbians and gay men and, as a consequence, many had their stereotypes dissolved.

There are many chronic sicknesses that impact on lesbians and gay men at the same rate as the rest of the population. Because HIV and AIDS has had a differential impact, it carries with it significant social meaning. Social workers must be equipped to work with chronic sickness, but in addition they need to be sensitive to the social meaning for lesbians and gay men of AIDS and HIV.

Death and bereavement have, since the early eighties, been dominating realities for lesbians and gay men. Among them it would be difficult to find a single person who has not been affected. Lesbians and gay men die and are bereaved for the same reasons as the rest of the population, but in addition they have been hit disproportionately by the AIDS epidemic. Despite all the death and bereavement, there has been little recognition of this by mainstream services, most provision coming from autonomous organisations. Although the provision by these organisations is welcomed, sensitive social work and health services need to be available within the mainstream to provide an appropriate service to a dying lesbian or gay man and their family, lovers and friends, and to bereaved lesbians and gay men.

Physical disability

The subject of gender and disability has attracted some consideration (Campling, 1981; Morris, 1989, 1993; Lonsdale, 1990: Begum, 1992), but that of sexual-orientation and disability has attracted very little (GLC and the GLC Gay Working Party, 1985; GLC, 1986; Hearn, 1991). However, absence from the literature is not reflected by any absence of activity in the community. In the British context, lesbian and gay disabled people have been engaged in both formal and informal organisations for a long time, including conferences for disabled lesbians and gay men, and the setting up of Lesbians and Gays United in Disability (LANGUID), an umbrella group for disabled lesbian and gay organisations; but quite what impact this has had on the provision of social work services is debatable.

Most disabled lesbians and gay men have minimal contact with social work organisations and most will have none. However, we can assume that there are a significant number of disabled lesbians and gay men who are in receipt of either social work intervention or provision or both. Hearn talks about the marginalisation of disabled lesbians and gay men, both from the disability movement and from lesbian and gay communities. There are many stereotypes surrounding disabled people, one of the most prevalent being asexuality; where a person is recognised as having a sexuality at all, it is usually assumed to be heterosexual.

Disabled lesbians and gay men are not a homogeneous group and each individual needs to be listened to in relation to their experience, needs and wants. Disabled lesbians and gay men may be in contact with social work agencies for entirely different reasons, quite apart from their disability, for example childcare needs. Assessment, and the provision of homecare services, day facilities and residential provision are all social work provisions that need to be sensitive to the needs of lesbians and gay men, to be open, able to listen and respond appropriately. ' "Coming out" can be extremely risky for lesbians dependent on heterosexist carers, whether they are family, friends or paid workers' (GLC, 1986: 8). Rethinking social work provision was considered in Chapter 6; this is particularly relevant here.

For disabled lesbians and gay men to benefit from resources that may be made available to them from social work organisations, they have to feel comfortable enough about revealing who they are in their complex totality to the providers of those resources. If they feel that whole areas of their lives have to be concealed then the provision is likely to be ineffectual and may contribute considerable distress and stress. There has been substantial criticism of social work practice with disabled people (Oliver, 1983), it being argued that social work has pursued an 'individual tragedy' model in relation to disability. The problems facing disabled people are as much to do with the social construction of disability as with the individual's experience. Social work with the individual in their social context, including their political context, needs to remain sensitive to the personal as well as the social. Disability for some individuals is indeed a 'tragedy'. The loss of both legs in an accident might well initially be experienced by some people as a personal tragedy. Never being able to pick your child up may be experienced as a personal tragedy. To deny individuals the right to experience their own responses to any given set of such circumstances would be insensitive, dehumanising and oppressive. Social work, in addressing the individual within their own context, should be able to deliver a non-oppressive and non-patronising service to disabled lesbians and gay men, which both respects individuals' experiences and responses and also can locate them within a broader social and political context.

Old age

Old age is a social construction: it is not, by itself, a reason for social work intervention. Old people are sometimes in need of social work intervention because of other related matters, which are often to do with disability. Old people are affected by society's attitudes to ageing, which in western white cultures is nearly exclusively negative. Ageism has major impacts on individuals, influencing service provision, perceptions of old people and their perceptions of themselves. There has been some consideration of the relationship between gender and ageing (Finch and Groves, 1985; Hemmings, 1985; Ford and Sinclair, 1987; Arber and Ginn, 1991; Hughes and Mtezuka, 1992) as well as that between sexual-orientation and ageing (Kelly, 1977; Weeks, 1981; Berger, 1990; Brown, 1992a; Gibson, 1992; Tully, 1992; Seneviratne, 1995).

Older lesbians and gay men have particular areas of vulnerability as well as possible strengths that they may have developed through managing to survive in a homophobic society. These strengths may be transferable to coping with ageism. Brown contextualises the position of older lesbians within the social realities facing older women generally, both in terms of both financial vulnerability and bereavement, the second being equally relevant to gay men. Older women are vulnerable financially, and make up a significant proportion of the very poor, their financial provision having often been related to their employment history but mainly to the employment status of their husbands (Finch and Groves, 1985):

> Some older lesbians will have been or may still be married, but many will have remained 'single', or lived with other women, whose earning capacities – in the main – will not have been equivalent to those of men. Social workers will therefore need to keep lesbian clients' economic circumstances in mind, as they may suffer disproportionate hardship. (Brown, 1992a: 212)

Bereavement is a familiar aspect of many old people's lives, and some people will be in need of skilled intervention to assist them to cope with it. Lesbians and gay men, as mentioned before, can experience additional pressures associated with bereavement:

> As their relationships are unrecognised by law, they are vulnerable in relation to joint property. They may never have openly acknowledged their relationship, and be ignored or even openly resented by families. They may feel there is nowhere sympathetic to go to talk through their loss. (Brown, 1992a: 212)

Social work is renowned for its poor counselling provision to older people generally, and lesbians and gay men may not be 'visible' to the profession and may therefore be a particularly vulnerable group in respect of bereavement.

Gibson reflects on the extreme stereotyping of old gay men:

> There is an unkind and largely false stereotype of the 'aged queen' or 'auntie', a man who is presumed to have had many homosexual contacts when he was young and good-looking, but in later life finds it impossible to attract sexual partners and is consequently lonely and miserable. This stereotype is not held only by the 'straight' (heterosexual) majority, but it is believed by many of the younger homosexual generation. (Gibson, 1992: 152)

Berger also comments on the extreme stereotypes of old lesbians and gay men:

these stereotypes have had a devastating effect on all gays and lesbians, young and old. They have been used to discourage gay people from accepting themselves, and they have wrought havoc on their self-concepts. (Berger, 1990: 171)

Gibson argues that a large number of gay men are likely to be in touch with health and social work provision because, in the main, they do not have the wives and daughters who make up the usual army of informal carers, and are therefore more likely than hetero-sexual men to be in need of formal support and care. Berger has noted the paucity of material relevant to the ageing of lesbians and gay men and is forced to ask, 'Do gay men and lesbians self-destruct at the age of forty?' (1990: 170). What research there is rebuffs many of the stereotypes; for example, older lesbians, rather than being particularly lonely or desperate, are in fact more likely than older heterosexual women to use non-familial informal networks.

Old lesbians and gay men, having lived through very oppressive times, may have developed strengths that are transferable to coping with the oppression associated with ageing. Stigma is something that both old people and lesbians and gay men experience. Berger argues that the skills that are developed by lesbians and gay men in younger life are then used to combat the ageism and resulting stigma they experience in older life. 'The advantage for gays and lesbians is that they have learned how to cope with a stigmatised identity very early in life' (1990: 173).

Because many lesbians and gay men do not have the support of their birth families, there is a reliance on informal networks of care and friendship. This may be a particular strength for people as they get older. Social workers need to acknowledge these networks and involve them when making assessments of the needs of an old person. However, they should never make the assumption that they exist.

Brown has discussed the possible strength for older lesbians in often having adopted less rigid gender-roles throughout their devel-opment:

Another possible area of strength is role flexibility (Berger and Kelly, 1986). Lesbians are more likely to have had more equal domestic relationships than heterosexual women, and may well be skilled in a wider range of domestic responsibilities, whether they have lived with others, with partners, or alone. If they are bereaved, they may be in a stronger position to continue with day-to-day existence, cooking, changing fuses, paying bills. (Brown, 1992a: 213)

Social work has sometimes approached working with oppressed groups with the assumption of a victim status on behalf of the recipient. In the 'exchange model' social workers need to be identifying strengths the clients/service users already have that can be built upon at the same time as not denying weakness and vulnerability.

Learning disabilities

Ryan and Thomas offer us an excellent history of the oppression of people with learning disabilities (1987). They argue that this history is partly to do with the changing definitions of difference:

The changing definitions of difference constitute the history of mentally handicapped people. These definitions have been conceived of by others, never are they the expression of a group of people finding their own identity, their own history. The assertion of difference between people is seldom neutral; it almost always implies some kind of social distance or distinction. (Ryan and Thomas, 1987: 13)

Since the setting up of People First in Britain in 1984, along the lines of its counterparts in America, a start has been made to make some inroads in enabling learning-disabled people to find their own voice, definitions and identity. However, the vast majority of learning-disabled people are still subject to other people's perception of them and anxieties about them. One of the key areas of anxiety has been sex. There has been much helpful material developed in this area in relation to lesbians and gay men as well as heterosexuals (Craft, 1994; Turk and Brown, 1992; McCarthy and Thompson, 1992; McCarthy and Thompson, 1994; Thompson, 1994).

McCarthy and Thompson, in their excellent training package for staff (1992), point out two important areas that need to be kept in mind. First, same-sex activity does not necessarily lead to the participant perceiving themselves to be gay. Same-sex activity is prevalent among men who identify as heterosexual and this applies no less with learning-disabled people. Second, the levels of same-sex activity among women seems to be significantly lower than in the rest of the population:

> Women having sex with women is, in the authors' experience, the least common form of sexual expression among people with learning difficulties . . . There seem to be two possible explanations for this, either there are very few women with learning difficulties who have sex with other women, or this kind of sexual behaviour is taking place, but it is unacknowledged or unseen. (McCarthy and Thompson, 1992: 43)

These authors stress the importance of carers being open to people talking about same-sex sexual activity because the person will need to feel confident of getting a non-prejudiced response. This has been particularly relevant in relation to the dissemination of information to men about safer sex. Thompson's findings, arising out of direct work with men with learning disabilities in the context of a hospital-based sex education project, are fairly depressing:

> It is important to remember that a passive, compliant and, on occasion, painful experience of sex with men was commonplace among the men with learning disabilities. Their reasons for having sex with men cannot be easily attributed to either sexual preference or sexual pleasure. Although these experiences appear to be negative, many men, most noticeably those who hung around public toilets, were very active in seeking out such encounters. Definitely, these sexual contacts might have offered men incidental sexual pleasure but other incentives have emerged which have nothing to do with sexuality. These include being a way to fill time with few other options, a small financial or material gain, and an exchange for the valued attention of men without learning disabilities. (Thompson, 1994: 262)

Same-sex activity is not synonymous with a homosexual identity. We are learning more about the nature of the same-sex activity but little about people with learning disabilities who identify as lesbians and gay men.

Work with adults who are lesbian or gay requires competence. In addition to the areas that we normally subsume under 'competence' there may be additional considerations in relation to specific areas of work. Social work, lesbian and gay individuals and communities are all dynamic entities. These considerations should not be fixed or assumed but should be open to change and development resulting from an awareness of the relevant literature and, most importantly, from conversation with clients/service users.

9

Social Work and Probation Practice with Offenders

Much that has gone before in this book is relevant to work with offenders within the criminal justice system. Lesbians and gay men are subject to the same ideologies and practices here as they have been in other areas of social work practice. Issues in relation to the theoretical base of social work, organisational contexts, and lesbians and gay men as both workers and clients are equally relevant to the organisational contexts within which offenders are worked with. How we work with offenders – the structures, controlling statutes, processes and practices – will be dictated by the national location and the organisational context. This chapter does not address itself to the detail of work with offenders within the criminal justice system, but rather concentrates on areas that are worthy of reflection when trying to develop anti-oppressive practice with lesbians and gay men in this specific context. The chapter reflects on work with both adult and young offenders. With regard to juvenile justice and young lesbians and gay men, it should be considered in conjunction with the section on young people in Chapter 7. Civil work is not covered here, as the relevant areas in relation to children and families are covered in Chapter 6.

The British criminal justice system

Lesbians and gay men are caught up in the criminal justice system for the same complex reasons as other people. They may, however, figure additionally in the statistics for quite different reasons.

It has been argued that gay men are in a disadvantaged position within the criminal justice system (NAPO, 1989, 1990; Ford and Robinson, 1993; Gocke, 1995; Denney, 1996); this is largely because of the criminalisation of aspects of gay male sex. The legislation does not directly concern itself with male homosexual identity, but with specific matters relating to sex. A significant number of men prosecuted under the legislation will identify as heterosexual, but a disproportionate number will identify as gay. The sexual matters that the legislation makes illegal are associated with gay male sexual practices, and can therefore be seen as a mechanism for the social control of an oppressed group. The relevant laws, 'though not naming or stipulating gay men, are almost invariably used by police to "control" the "picking-up" of gay men by other gay men' (GLC and the GLC Gay Working Party, 1985: 35). The nearest British law has come in legislation relating to lesbian and gay identity is section 28 of the Local Government Act 1988. Two seventeen-year-old young men engaged in sexual activity are breaking the law. They may in other respects in no way be considered as 'offenders' but because they are gay men and aspects of gay male sex are criminalised they have fallen foul of the law. Ford and Robinson list offences relevant to gay men that do not affect heterosexuals:

(i)   Prohibition on consensual sex between the ages of 16 and 21. [as noted in Chapter 3 these have now become 16 and 18.]

(ii)   Soliciting of one man by another in a public place – unlike female prostitution this does not have to involve money and may therefore simply be 'chatting up' by gay men in the street.

(iii)   Procuring of homosexual acts – this could include a man allowing two consenting male friends to stay overnight at his home, or introducing two male friends to each other (matchmaking), etc.

(iv)   Indecency between men – this can include kissing and hugging in a park, etc.

. . . This inequality continues to lead to discrimination against gay men. In particular s.31 of the Criminal Justice Act 1991 lists offences (ii)–(iv) as sexual offences allowing for the use of custody at a lower threshold than applied to other offences under s.1(2). Consensual gay sex 'offences' are transformed into 'serious sexual offences' on a par with child abuse. (Ford and Robinson, 1993: 12)

It could be argued that this legislation does not just 'lead' to discrimination: it actively sanctions it. Ford and Robinson have not included here the importance of the distinction between 'private' and 'public', which impacts on gay men (see Chapter 3). Gay men working in the criminal justice system will find themselves working with other gay men who have been defined as criminal for doing things that the workers are doing themselves and that it would be unusual not to do as a sexually active person. One person is defined as a criminal and one is not, by pure chance.

It has long been recognised that gender and race impact on offending behaviour, arrests, sentencing and treatment within the criminal justice system. This has been recognised in section 95 of the Criminal Justice Act 1991, in relation to both gender and race (Home Office, 1992a; Home Office, 1992b). There has been no such public recognition of the position of lesbians and gay men. The Act places a duty on the criminal justice system not to discriminate, while at the same time the Act adds to the active discrimination against and oppression of gay men.

Raising the issues concerning the discrimination of lesbians and gay men has been left almost exclusively to lesbian and gay workers within the probation service. Most 'radical' probation texts make no mention of the difficulties encountered by lesbians and gay men (Walker and Beaumont, 1981); neither do mainstream probation texts (such as Walker and Beaumont, 1985; May, 1991; Statham and Whitehead, 1992; Raynor *et al.*, 1994; Osler, 1995; May and Vass, 1996), with the notable exceptions of Worrall (1995) (which does not directly address lesbian and gay concerns but is no less applicable), Gocke (1995), Padel (1995) and Denney (1996). The most detailed material in this area has developed out of the National Association of Probation Officers (NAPO), as a response to the work of Lesbians and Gays in Probation (LAGIP), which was formed in 1983. Their focus, similar to lesbian and gay activity within NALGO and UNISON, has been to work simultaneously for better service conditions for lesbians and gay men and for the bettering of the quality of probation intervention and service delivery to lesbian and gay clients/offenders. They have a network throughout England and Wales, and organise national conferences. There have also been a number of relevant texts to come out of Sheffield Hallam University (Senior and Woodhill, 1992; McCaughey and Buckley, 1993).

Much has been written about women offenders and their treatment within the criminal justice system (Carlen, 1990; Worrall, 1990; NACRO, 1991; Eaton, 1993; Smart, 1995), and we can assume that a great deal of what is considered to apply to women offenders generally will also be relevant to lesbians. Some aspects, however, may be made more extreme by a woman's lesbianism. Eaton, looking at the experiences of women in prison, notes the following:

> Certainly most women experienced rule enforcement as capricious and focused particularly on women who did not conform to an expected or appropriate behaviour pattern. Any variation from this extreme version of a gender stereotype is treated with suspicion . . . Such victimisation of those who manifest an unacceptable demeanour is particularly noticeable in cases where women's sexuality transgresses, or poses a threat to, traditional gender roles. Lesbianism constitutes a major challenge since it constructs women without reference to men . . . By creating a taboo (lesbian activity) the prison authorities undermine not only women-directed sexuality but also other manifestations of solidarity and support among the women. (Eaton, 1993: 27–8)

The discrimination that impacts on lesbians and gay men caught up in the criminal justice system impacts on probation practice both within prisons and in the community. Gay men are criminalised because of aspects of their sexual practice and it would seem that perceptions of lesbians as non-conforming women may impact on their experiences once arrested. Lesbians and gay men are not only involved in the criminal justice system for these reasons. They also commit offences that are separate from their sexuality and need to be treated as such. Separating out the offence from the person's sexual-orientation where it is irrelevant is an essential component of competent practice within probation.

Community-based probation and resources

Probation practice in the British context is regulated by National Standards for the supervision of offenders in the community (Home Office, Department of Health and Welsh Office, 1995). Included in the tasks performed by probation officers is the production of Pre-

Sentence Reports (PSRs). This requires the probation officer to assess the following: an 'analysis of the offence'; the 'context in which the offence occurred'; the 'impact on the victim'; the 'offender's attitude to the victim and offence and awareness of its consequences'; and, lastly:

> assessment of the implications of any special circumstances, e.g. family crisis, which were directly relevant to the offending, drawing attention to any ways in which they may be relevant to the court's judgements of its seriousness. (1995: 10)

In relation to this last point, in preparing a PSR on a gay man before the courts for 'soliciting', it would be tempting to point out that the only reason the man is before the court is that the law itself is problematic, in being discriminatory. This is a victimless crime – sex between two consenting adults. The 'points to keep in mind during an assessment' (Chapter 6) and the 'aspects' of discrimination (Chapter 6) are as relevant here as to other areas of social work practice. If someone feels, or has actually been, criminalised because of their sexual-orientation, they may have particular concerns about being 'assessed' or their offence being assessed by an officer of the court. NAPO make the following comments in relation to the preparation of PSRs for lesbian and gay offenders:

> Prejudice is rife in Courts and officers who know about a client's sexual orientation and feel it to be relevant either to offending behaviour or to arguments about discrimination hesitate to mention the matter . . . In reports, information about sexual orientation should invariably be accompanied by explanations of discrimination and how that will have affected the client's behaviour: attempts should be made to explain and counteract the pathologising of gayness . . . Where it is felt that the disclosure of a client's lesbian or gay identity would push them up the tariff, report writers should include an explanation of the prejudicial attitudes and discrimination experienced by the offender in order to counteract this possibility. (NAPO, 1989: 3)

NAPO also suggest that the sexuality of the offender should only be mentioned if it is directly relevant to the offence. They are suggesting, sensibly, that both the offence and the homosexuality of the client, where relevant, should be contextualised into the wider political and social realities of oppression and homophobia. How this is to be done effectively requires skill and diplomacy, or the result could be an exhibition in political posturing that is likely to do more harm to the offender's case than good. Probation officers who wish for social justice to be done, which would require changes in the legislation relevant to gay male sexual practice, need to channel their energies through appropriate and effective avenues and not be tempted to use the court in a way that would be detrimental to the offender.

Supervision of lesbian and gay offenders in the community will involve the same need, as has been discussed earlier, of placing considerable emphasis on the process of engagement, in order to enable sufficient trust to be established. There may be areas that someone does want to work around that may be directly relevant to their offence and their sexuality, but they will be unable to do this unless they feel that their sexual-orientation is viewed as a valid sexual choice and that they are respected and valued. Unless this trust is established, we force people into defensive positions or over-compliance.

Probation officers need access to information about resources and organisations that are relevant to lesbians and gay men so that they can help direct the client/offender into an appropriate network or put them in touch with helping resources where this is helpful. The role of the probation officer in the supervision of offenders needs to include the facilitation of skills development by the client/offender in order to find their way around and through the criminal justice system which, within its different contexts, is not renowned for its sympathy towards lesbians and gay men.

There are a number of sentence outcomes that will direct an offender to alternatives to custody that are located in the community (Vass, 1990). These alternatives need to be welcoming to all their recipients. Ford and Robinson have addressed the question of the appropriateness and relevance of some sex offender programmes to gay men. They argue that sex offenders are often seen as a heterosexual, homogeneous group, and that this ignores the specific needs of some of them (1993). An individual's sex offence might be directly related to ambivalence towards or negative feelings about homosexuality; to fully explore this in the context of a sex offender programme needs skilled facilitation and interventions from the workers if sufficient trust is to be engendered within the group for this kind of complex work to have a positive resolution. To help a lesbian or gay man feel included may need a proactive approach as well as the examination of the provision as outlined in Chapter 6, to enable the alternative to prison to be a real alternative for lesbian and gay offenders.

Residential provision – prisons and hostels

Sex between men in a 'public' place or with a third person present is against the law in Britain (see Chapter 3). The 'private' circumstances in which it is legal for gay men to have consensual sex, as long as they are over eighteen, are defined as excluding hotels, prisons or hostels (Buckley, 1992). The implications of this for hostel workers are immense. Social workers have always had to find a way of steering their way round the age of consent for both gay men and heterosexuals, but hostel staff, as with staff at any residential establishment, do need guidance generally in relation to sex between residents. Unless this guidance is available, there tends to be a panic response if there is a problem or a controversy, which is rarely in the resident's interests. Lloyd refers to the bullying of gay men in hostels (1993) as being a considerable problem. Hostels need clear guidance and procedures on how to deal with all types of harassment, and people coming into those hostels need to be made aware that harassment will not be tolerated. NAPO makes the same point: 'Discrimination is widespread and harassment goes unchallenged'. The same text goes on to suggest that NAPO members involved in this provision 'should attempt to develop regimes which do not tolerate heterosexist behaviour' (1989: 4). The use of language is a little unfortunate here. Regimes suppress; they are not renowned for their ability to facilitate change. It is possible to be clear about acceptable and non-acceptable behaviour without making people's home, for that is what it is for whatever their period of residence, into a 'regime'.

It is difficult to draw conclusions as to the quality of lesbians' lives in hostels on the basis of gay men's experience. I can only draw on my own experience as a social worker working jointly with the probation service in relation to two women's hostels where our involvement was with lesbian clients. Neither of the two women involved experienced bullying or harassment within those contexts. Both women, however, were perceived as being powerful. Ourselves and the hostel staff, were engaged in a complex assessment of one lesbians' parenting over a number of months. The positive outcome of that work would not have been possible if she had experienced the hostel as excluding and hostile. We do not know the numbers of lesbians employed as workers in hostels, but in my limited experience the prevalence of lesbians in hostel work is visible: this may be a contributory factor among many others in the apparent possibility that lesbians and gay men experience different qualities of life within hostels.

'In prisons homosexuality is defined as illegal and lesbianism is defined as an offence against "good order and discipline"' (NAPO, 1989: 4). The issues surrounding AIDS and HIV in prisons are most relevant to intravenous drug users (Padel, 1995), but the fear of AIDS has increased hostility towards gay prisoners (NAPO, 1989). Probation officers, both within prisons and working outside, need to take cognisance of the particular vulnerabilities that gay prisoners may experience. Sable, looking at lesbians and gay men in prison in America, talks about the difficulty of coming out in such a potentially hostile context, for those prisoners whose sexuality is not known. If gay men opt for protective custody, there are often associated losses: for example, less access to educational opportunities. Sable comments on the experiences of violence perpetrated on gay men:

> While sexual victimisation is not limited to gay-identified men in a prison population, such men are preferential targets of such violence and exploitation and they are over represented in the numbers of those who are so abused. (Sable, 1990: 186)

Prison sentences may have serious implications for gay men. Probation officers need to be proactive in monitoring the progression of gay prisoners throughout their detention.

Competent anti-oppressive practice in work with offenders

The Probation Training Unit of the Home Office has produced a booklet identifying probation competencies. These competencies include the following areas that I consider relevant to working with lesbians and gay men:

> The service . . . acknowledges the differences between individuals in a positive way and promotes services which build on these strengths . . . Working to tackle discrimination, Staff aim to:
> – treat all service users fairly, openly and with respect;
> – achieve equality of opportunity throughout the service and all its activities through access to training and progression;
> – promote and maintain anti-discriminatory practice;
> – support each other in work activities and treat each other fairly, openly and with respect. (1994: 3–4)

These declarations, if put into practice, would guarantee the security and inclusion of lesbians and gay men as clients/offenders and workers alike. There are contradictory factors that probation officers have to live with and find ways to manage in working with lesbians and gay men. Laws that gay men may be arrested under in relation to their sexual practice are fundamentally oppressive, and probation officers are officers of the courts in which those gay men are sentenced. They are, nevertheless, expected to offer an anti-discriminatory service to gay men who have been made criminal through the administration of anti-gay laws. However, contradictions often lead to creativity. Many probation officers do offer a competent service delivery to lesbians and gay men, irrespective of the contradictory nature of their position. They can facilitate a client coping with their involvement with the criminal justice system and offer a respectful, trusting and constructive working relationship to facilitate clients/offenders making the best possible use of their probation order.

10

Concluding Thoughts

Social work with lesbians and gay men takes place in a political and social context that inevitably impacts on practice. There have been considerable political and social movements and events that have affected both lesbian and gay communities and social work. Resulting changes, some of them contradictory, have opened up the possibility for social workers, their agencies, and social work educational establishments to re-evaluate their service delivery to lesbian and gay individuals and communities.

Social work knowledge

The relationship between knowledge, values and skills is complex and entwined. They need to be considered independently and in relationship to each other. Three areas of knowledge were identified in Chapter 5 (p. 57), namely:

> knowledge that informs the practitioner about the client's experience and context; knowledge that helps the practitioner plan appropriate intervention; and knowledge that clarifies the practitioner's understanding of the legal, policy, procedural and organisational context in which their practice takes place. (Brown, 1996: 10),

These need to be reviewed as to their impact on and relevance to lesbian and gay clients/service users. Rethinking social work practice with lesbians and gay men necessitates a revaluation of all three areas. It requires us to re-evaluate social work knowledge in terms of its prejudicial impact on lesbians and gay men and to contextualise the knowledge base, within its historical, social, economic and cultural context. Lesbians and gay men should benefit from the richness of ideas available to practitioners, while at the same time social workers need to apply their own critical thinking as to its relevance to the delivery of competent practice.

In addition, social workers are professionally responsible for seeking out specific knowledge that will be relevant to working with lesbians and gay men. For example, a social worker who is undertaking an assessment of the possible delayed development of a child whose mother is a lesbian should avail themselves of relevant research material in relation to outcomes of child development for children of lesbians. This will help the worker be better informed during the assessment and benefit not only the child but also the quality of the worker's contribution to multidisciplinary discussions and decision-making. Social work organisations will improve the quality of their service by keeping an updated list of relevant agencies, networks and resources that would be useful to practitioners and lesbians and gay men who are clients/service users.

Social work education

Social work education is one of the major vehicles through which social work knowledge is imparted. Both in the design of curricula and the processes of imparting that knowledge, consideration needs to be given to the above when thinking about future service delivery to 'clients' and whether all potential service users are equally kept in mind. Social work education is also the main vehicle of initiation into the profession of social work. The processes that lesbian and gay students experience through this 'initiation' will have implications as to how included they feel within the profession, and what contributions they feel they can make in the future. This is relevant to both the college context and the social work placement experience. Practice teachers on placements need to be aware of the possible experiences for lesbians and gay men going through the process of social work education and be open and appropriately supportive (Inner London Probation Service, 1993; Logan *et al.*, 1996).

The educational process is important. For many people, it will be their first formal contact with social work organisations wherein they are holding the formal role of social worker. Their experiences are likely to have a lasting impact, and will affect lesbian and gay students' degree of confidence as future practitioners. The social work educational process can also convey a message to heterosexual and homosexual students about the degree of value that the profession places on the quality of social work provision to lesbians and gay men.

Social work practice

Competent practice requires the following abilities:

- to be able to draw on applicable knowledge;
- to be able to evaluate that knowledge;
- to be able to consider the relevant values not only of the worker and client/service user but also of their immediate system, agency and the legislative framework, in relation to specific pieces of work;
- to be able to utilise necessary skills.

Social workers also need the capacity to reflect upon their own and their organisations' quality of service delivery with the intention of facilitating change where necessary to better the outcome for clients/service users.

Practice considerations include:

- the quality of direct service delivery, whether of social work interventions, assessment or provision of a service or services;
- the quality of supervision;
- the 'culture' of the organisation, and whether it is welcoming and inclusive of diversity.

Lesbians and gay men who are either in need of or in receipt of social work interventions and services have the right to a relevant, appropriate, welcoming, inclusive, facilitative and competent anti-oppressive service delivery. Social workers, together with their agencies, and their educators, as well as clients/service users themselves, have begun the processes required to achieve the changes and developments necessary for us to reach the point of being able to consistently deliver such a service. Some individuals and agencies have been engaged in these processes for a very long time. This book is one contribution towards the conversations that must be had on this journey to ensure that, when we engage with or intervene in the lives of lesbians and gay men, our interventions and the services we provide are competent.

Relevant Organisations

The Albert Kennedy Trust
23 New Mount Street,
Manchester
M4 4DE
Tel: 0161 953 5049

Black Lesbian and Gay Centre Project
BM Box 4390
London
WC1N 3XX

FFLAG – Families and Friends of Lesbians and Gays
Co-ordinator
PO Box 153
Manchester
M60 1LP

Galop – Gay London Policing Group
Tel: 0171 233 0854

Glad (legal advice)
Tel: 0171 976 0840

Helplines
Lesbian Line 0171 251 6911

Bisexual Helpline   **London** 0181 569 7500
                       Edinburgh 0131 557 3620

Black Lesbian and Gay Helpline 0171 837 5364

Friend 0171 837 3337

Lesbian and Gay Switchboard 0171 837 7324

Irish Gay Helpline
BM Box IGH
London, WC1N 3XX

Tel: 0181 983 4111

Jewish Lesbian and Gay Helpline
BM Box 2585
London
WC1N 3XX

Tel: 0171 706 3123

Lesbian and Gay Bereavement Project
Vaughan M Williams Centre
Colindale Hospital
London
NW9 5HG

Tel: 0181 200 0511

Lesbian and Gay Carers Campaign
50 Southwark Street
London
SE1 1UN

Tel: 0171 226 1824

Lesbian and Gay Christian Movement
Oxford House
Derbyshire Street
London
E2 6HG

Tel:0171 587 1235

Lesbian and Gay Disability Group

Tel: 0121 459 5859

Lesbian and Gay Fostering and Adoptive Parents' Group,
c/o London Friend
86, Caledonian Road
London
N1

Lesbian Custody Project, Rights of Women
52, Featherstone Street
London
EC1Y 8RT

Tel: 0171 251 9951

Manchester L and G Disabled Group
Manchester Gay Centre
Sydney Street
P O Box 153
Manchester

Tel: 0161 274 3814

PACE – Project for Advice Counselling and Education
34 Hartham Road
London
N7 9JL

Tel: 0171 700 1323

Parentline
Rayfa House
57 Hart Road
Thundersley
Essex
SS7 3PD

Tel: 01268 757077

Parent Network
44–46 Caversham Road
London
NW5 2DS

Tel: 0171 485 8535

Positive Parenting Campaign
Dept 7
1 Newton Street
Manchester
M1 1HW

Quest – Gay Catholic Group
BM Box 2585
London
WC1N 3XX

Tel: 0171 792 0234

Regard
For Lesbians and Gay Men With Disabilities
88 Maidstone Road
London
N11 2JR

Shakti
South Asian Lesbian and Gay Network
BM Box 3167
London
WC1N 3XX

Stonewall Parenting Group
c/o Stonewall
16 Clerkenwell Close
London
EC1R 0AA

Tel: 0171 336 8860

Streetwise Youth
11 Eardley Crescent
Earls Court
London
SW5 9JS

Tel: 0171 370 0037

A useful directory of lesbian and gay organisations is *Cassell's 1994 Pink Directory: Lesbian and Gay Organisations, Businesses and Services in the UK and Eire*, London: Cassell.

References

Adams, R. (1990) *Self-Help, Social Work and Empowerment*, Basingstoke: Macmillan.

Ahmad, B. (1990) *Black Perspectives in Social Work*, Birmingham: Venture Press.

Albert Kennedy Trust (1995) *The Albert Kennedy Trust: General Information Guide*, Manchester: Albert Kennedy Trust.

Ali, T. (1996) *We Are Family: Testimonies of Lesbian and Gay Parents*, London: Cassell.

Anti-Discrimination Board of NSW (1994a) *1993/1994 Annual Report*, Sydney: Anti-Discrimination Board of NSW.

Anti-Discrimination Board of NSW (1994b) *Homosexual Discrimination – Your Rights*, Sydney: Anti-Discrimination Board.

Arber, S. and Ginn, J. (1991) *Gender and Later Life: A Sociological Analysis of Resources and Constraints*, London: Sage.

Arnup, K. (ed.) (1995) *Lesbian Parenting: Living with Pride and Prejudice*, Charlottetown, Canada: Gynergy Books.

Ashurst, P. and Hall, Z. (1989) *Understanding Women in Distress*, London: Tavistock/Routledge.

AUT [Association of University Teachers] (1991) *Sexual Orientation and Employment in the Universities*, LA/4227a/Feb 1991, London: AUT.

Baistow, K. (1995) 'Liberation and Regulation? Some Paradoxes of Empowerment', *Critical Social Policy*, vol. 14, no. 3, pp. 34–46.

Barclay, P. M. (1982) *Social Workers: Their Role and Tasks*, London: National Institute of Social Work/Bedford Square Press.

Barrett, M. and McIntosh, M. (1982) *The Anti-Social Family*, London: Verso.

BASW [British Association of Social Work] (1988) *A Code of Ethics for Social Work*, London: BASW.

Begum, M. (1992) 'Disabled Women and the Feminist Agenda', *Feminist Review*, no. 40, pp. 70–84.

Beresford, P. and Croft, S. (1993) *Citizen Involvement: A Practical Guide for Change*, London: Macmillan.

Berger, R. M. (1990) 'Older Gays and Lesbians', in R. J. Kus (ed.), *Keys to Caring: Assisting Your Gay and Lesbian Clients*, Boston: Alyson Publications. pp. 170–81.

Berger, R. M. and Kelly, J. J. (1986) 'Working with homosexuals of the older population', *Social Casework*, vol. 67, no. 4, pp. 203–10.

Biestek, F. P. (1957) *The Casework Relationship*, Chicago: Loyola University Press.

Boston Lesbian Psychologies Collective (eds) (1987) *Lesbian Psychologies*, Chicago: University of Illinois Press.

Bowl, R. and Barnes, M. (1990) 'Race, Racism and Mental Health Social Work: Implications for Local Authority Policy and Training', *Research, Policy and Planning*, vol. 2, no. 2, pp. 12–18.

Bowlby, J. (1988) *A Secure Base. Clinical Applications of Attachment Theory*, London: Routledge.

Boyd, C., Doyle, D., Foley, B., Harvey, B., Hoctor, A., Molloy, M. and Quinlan, M. (eds) (1986) *Out For Ourselves. The Lives of Irish Lesbians and Gay Men*, Dublin: Dublin Lesbian and Gay Men's Collective.

Bozett, F. W. (1982) 'Heterogenous Couples in Heterosexual Marriages: Gay Men and Straight Women', *Journal of Marital and Family Therapy*, vol. 8, pp. 81–89.

Bozett, F. W. (1987) 'Children of Gay Fathers', in F. W. Bozett (ed.), *Gay and Lesbian Parents*, New York: Praeger, pp. 39–57.

Bozett, F. W. (1989a) *Homosexuality and the Family*, New York: Harrington Park Press.

Bozett, F. W. (1989b) 'Gay Fathers: A Review of the Literature', in F. W. Bozett (ed.), *Homosexuality and the Family*, New York: Harrington Park Press, pp. 137–62.

Bozett, F. W. and Sussman, M. B. (eds) (1990) *Homosexuality and Family Relations*, New York: Harrington Park Press.

Brake, M. and Bailey, R. (eds) (1980) *Radical Social Work and Practice*, London: Edward Arnold.

Brandon, J. and Davis, M. (1979) *The Limits of Competence in Social Work: The Assessment of Marginal Students in Social Work*, vol. 9, no. 3, pp. 295–347.

Brook, E. and Davis, A. (eds) (1985) *Women, the Family and Social Work*, London: Tavistock.

Brosnan, J. (1996) *Lesbians Talk Detonating the Nuclear Family*, London: Scarlett Press.

Brown, H. C. (1990) *Lesbian and Gay Issues in Child Care Practice*, London: Middlesex University, unpublished.

Brown, H. C. (1991) 'Competent Child-Focused Practice: Working with Lesbian and Gay Carers', *Adoption and Fostering*, vol. 15, no. 2, pp. 11–17.

Brown, H. C. (1992a) 'Lesbians, the State and Social Work Practice', in M. Langan and L. Day (eds), *Women, Oppression and Social Work*. London: Routledge. pp. 201–219.

Brown, H. C. (1992b) 'Gender, Sex and Sexuality in the Assessment of Prospective Carers', *Adoption and Fostering*, vol. 16, no. 2, pp. 30–4.

Brown, H. C. (1996) 'The Knowledge Base of Social Work', in A. A. Vass (ed.), *Social Work Competences: Core Knowledge, Values and Skills*, London: Sage, pp. 8–35.

Brown, H. C. and Pearce, J. J. (1992) 'Good Practice in the Face of Anxiety: Social Work with Girls and Young Women', *Journal of Social Work Practice*, vol. 6, no. 2, pp. 159–65.

Buckley, K. (1992) 'Heterosexism, Power and Social Policy', in P. Senior and D. Woodhill (eds), *Gender, Crime and Probation Practice*, Sheffield: PAUIC Publications, pp. 35–43.

Burck, C. and Speed, B. (eds) (1995) *Gender, Power and Relationships*, London: Routledge.

Burnham, D. (1992) 'Social Work Roles in Local Community Organisation Experiences with Lesbian Women and Gay Men', in N. J. Woodman (ed.), *Lesbian and Gay Lifestyles: A Guide for Counseling and Education*, New York: Irvington, pp. 145–68.

Campion, M. J. (1995) *Who's Fit to Be a Parent?*, London: Routledge.

Campling, J. (1981) *Images of Ourselves: Women with Disabilities Talking*, London: Routledge & Kegan Paul.

Carew, R. (1979) 'The Place of Knowledge in Social Work Activity', *British Journal of Social Work*, vol. 9, no. 3, pp. 349–64.

Carlen, P. (1990) *Alternatives To Women's Imprisonment*, Milton Keynes: Open University Press.

Carter, V. (1992)'Abseil Makes the Heart Grow Fonder: Lesbian and Gay Campaigning Tactics and Section 28', in K. Plummer (ed.), *Modern Homosexualities*, London: Routledge, pp. 217–26.

Catalano, D. J. (1990) 'The Emerging Gay and Lesbian Hospice Movement', in R. J. Kus (ed), *Keys to Caring: assisting Your Gay and Lesbian Clients*, Boston: Alyson, pp. 321–9.

CCETSW [Central Council for Education and Training in Social Work] (1975) *Education and Training for Social Work: A Working Group Discussion Paper*, London: CCETSW.

CCETSW (1976) *Values in Social Work: A Discussion Paper Produced by the Working Party on the Teaching of Value Bases Of Social Work*, Paper 13, London: CCETSW.

CCETSW (1986) *Equal Opportunities*, London: CCETSW.

CCETSW (1989) *Improving Standards in Practice Learning*, London: CCETSW.

CCETSW (1991) *DipSW: Rules and Requirements for the Diploma in Social Work (Paper 30)*, 2nd edn. London: CCETSW.

CCETSW (1992) *HIV and AIDS in the Diploma in Social Work*, London: CCETSW.

CCETSW (1995) *DipSW: Rules and Requirements for the Diploma in Social Work (paper 30)*, revised edn. London: CCETSW.

Christopher, E. (1987) *Sexuality and Birth Control in Community Work*, 2nd edn, London: Tavistock.

Clark, C. L. and Asquith, S. (1985) *Social Work and Social Philosophy: A Guide for Practice*, London: Routledge & Kegan Paul.

Cole Wilson, O. and Allen, C. (1994) 'The Black Perspective', in E. Healey and A. Mason (eds), *Stonewall 25: The Making of the Lesbian and Gay Community in Britain*, London: Virago, pp. 122–36.

Colvin, M. and Hawksley, J. (1989) *Section 28: A Practical Guide to the Law and its Implications*, London: National Council for Civil Liberties.

Cooper, D. (1994) *Sexing the City. Lesbian and Gay Politics Within the Activist State*, London: Rivers Oram.

Corrigan, P. and Leonard, P. (1978) *Social Work Practice Under Capitalism: A Marxist Approach*, London: Macmillan.

Coulshed, V. (1990) *Management in Social Work,* London: Macmillan.

Coulshed, V. (1991) (2nd edn) *Social Work Practice: An Introduction,* Basingstoke: Macmillan.

Craft, A. (ed.) (1994) *Sexuality and Learning Disabilities*, London: Routledge.

Creith, E. (1996) *Undressing Lesbian Sex: Popular Images, Private Acts and Public Consequences*, London: Cassell.

Cruikshank, M. (1992) *The Gay and Lesbian Liberation Movement*, London: Routledge.

Crwydren, R. (1994) 'Welsh Lesbian Feminist: a Contradiction in Terms?', in J. Aaron, T. Rees, S. Betts and M. Vincentelli (eds), *Our Sisters' Land*, Cardiff: University of Wales Press, pp. 294–300.

Dale, J. and Foster, P. (1986) *Feminists and State Welfare*, London: Routledge & Kegan Paul.

Dalrymple, J. and Burke, B. (1995) *Anti-Oppressive Practice: Social Care and the Law*, Buckingham: Open University Press.

d'Ardenne, P. and Mahtani, A. (1989) *Transcultural Counselling In Action*, London: Sage.

Davis, L. (1993) *Sex and the Social Worker*, new edn, London: Janus Publishing Company.

Denney, D. (1996) 'Discrimination and Anti-Discrimination in Probation', in A. A. Vass and T. May (eds), *Working with Offenders: Issues, Contexts and Outcomes*, London: Sage, pp. 51–75.

Department of Health (1989) *Caring for People: Community Care in the Next Decade and Beyond*, London: HMSO.

Department of Health (1990) *Foster Placement: Guidance and regulation*, Consultation Paper No. 16, London: Department of Health.

Department of Health (1991a) *Child Abuse: A Study of Inquiry Reports 1980–1989*, London: HMSO.

Department of Health (1991b) *Care Management and Assessment: Practitioners Guide*, London: HMSO.

Department of Health (1991c) *The Children Act 1989: Guidance and Regulations, vol. 3. Family Placements*, London: HMSO.

Department of Health (1991d) *The Adoption Law Review Discussion Paper No. 3*, London: HMSO.

Department of Health (1991e) *Working Together Under the Children Act 1989: A Guide to Arrangements for Inter-Agency Co-operation for the Protection of Children from Abuse*, London: HMSO.

Department of Health (1993a) *Adoption: The Future*, London: HMSO.

Department of Health (1993b) *Code of Practice: Mental Health Act 1983*, London: HMSO.

Department of Health (1996) *Building Bridges: A guide to Arrangements for Inter-Agency Working for the Care and Protection of Severely Mentally Ill People*, London: Department of Health.

Dominelli, L. (1988) *Anti-Racist Social Work*, Basingstoke: Macmillan.

Dominelli, L. and McLeod, E. (1989) *Feminist Social Work*. London: Macmillan.

Dutton, J. and Kohli, R. (1996) 'The Core Skills of Social Work', in A. A. Vass (ed), *Social Work Competences: Core Knowledge, Values and Skills*, London: Sage, pp. 62–82.

Eaton, M. (1993) *Women After Prison*, Buckingham: Open University Press.

Edwards, T. (1992) 'The AIDS Dialectics: Awareness, Identity, Death and Sexual Politics', in K. Plummer (ed.), *Modern Homosexualities*, London: Routledge, pp. 151–9.

Egan, G. (1990) *The Skilled Helper*, (4th edn), Pacific Grove, California: Brooks/Cole.

Ejo, Y. (1994) 'Questioning Everything', in E. Healey and A. Mason (eds), *Stonewall 25: The Making of the Lesbian and Gay Community in Britain*, London: Virago, pp. 15–19.

Ellis, M. L. (1994) 'Lesbians, Gaymen and Psychoanalytic Training', *Free Associations*, vol. 4, no. 32, pp. 501–18.

Erikson, E. (1965) *Childhood and Society*, Harmondsworth: Penguin.

Fairbairn, W. (1952) *Psychoanalytic Studies of the Personality*, London: Tavistock.

Finch, J. and Groves, J. (1985) 'Old Girl, Old Boy: Gender Divisions in Social Work with the Elderly', in E. Brook and A. Davis (eds), *Women, the Family and Social Work*, London: Tavistock, pp. 92–114.

Finlay, R. and Reynolds, J. (1987) *Social Work and Refugees: A Handbook on Working with People in Exile in the UK*, Cambridge: National Extension College and Refugee Action.

Finkelhor, D. and Russell, D. (1984) 'Women as Perpetrators: Review of the Evidence', in D. Finkelhor (ed.), *Child Sexual Abuse: New Theory and Research*, New York: Free Press, pp. 171–87.

Ford, J. and Sinclair, P. (1987) *Sixty Years On: Women Talk About Old Age*, London: The Women's Press.

Ford, R. and Robinson, N. (1993) 'Gay Men: Discrimination Within the Criminal Law and Sex Offender Programmes', in C. McCaughey and C. Buckley (eds), *Sexuality, Youth Work and Probation Practice*, Sheffield: PAUIC Publications, pp. 11–20.

Forsythe, B. (1995) 'Discriminating in Social Work – An Historical Note', *British Journal of Social Work*, vol. 25, no. 1, pp. 1–16.

French, S. (1993) 'What's So Great About Independence?', in J. Swain, V. Finkelstein, S. French and M. Oliver (eds), *Disabling Barriers – Enabling Environments*. London: Sage. pp. 44–48.

Gagnon, J.H. and Simon, W. (1973) *Sexual Conduct: The Social Sources of Human Sexuality*, London: Hutchinson.

Gibson, A. (1991) 'Erikson's Life Cycle Approach to Development', in J. Lishman (ed), *Handbook of Theory for Practice Teachers in Social Work*, London: Jessica Kingsley, pp. 36–47.

Gibson, H. B. (1992) *The Emotional and Sexual Lives of Older People: A Manual for Professionals*, London: Chapman & Hall.

GLC [Greater London Council] (1986) *Danger: Heterosexism at work*, London: Spider Publications.

GLC and the GLC Gay Working Party (1985) *Changing the World: London Charter for Gay and Lesbian Rights,* London: Strategic Policy Unit.

Gocke, B. (1995) 'Working With People Who Have Committed Sexual Offences – What Values Underpin the Behaviour and What Value Base are We Using in Attempting to Address It?', in B. Williams (ed), *Probation Values*, Birmingham: Venture Press, pp. 171–86.

Golombok, S., Spencer, A. and Rutter, A. (1983) 'Children in Lesbian and Single Parent Households: Psychosexual and Psychiatric Appraisal', *Journal of Child Psychology and Psychiatry*, vol. 24. pp. 551–72

Gonsiorek, J.C. and Weinrich, J.D. (eds) (1991) *Homosexuality: Research Implications for Public Policy*, California: Sage.

Gooding, C. (1992) *Trouble With the Law/A Legal Handbook for Lesbians and Gay Men*, London: GMP Publishers.

Gottman, J. S. (1990) 'Children of Gay and Lesbian Parents', in F. W. Bozett and M. B. Sussman (eds), *Homosexuality and Family Relations*, New York: Harrington Park Press, pp. 177–96.

Green, R. (1978) 'Sexual Identity of 37 Children Raised by Homosexual or Transexual Parents', *American Journal of Psychiatry*, vol. 135, no. 6, pp. 692–7.

Green, R., Mandel, J. B., Hotvedt, M. E., Gray, J., and Smith, L. (1986) 'Lesbian Mothers and Their Children: A Comparison with Soloparent Heterosexual Mothers and Their Children', *Archives of Sexual Behaviour*, vol. 15, pp. 167–84.

Greene, B. and Herek, G. M. (eds) (1994) *Lesbian and Gay Psychology: Theory, Research, and Clinical Applications*, London: Sage.

Groth, A. N. and Birnbaum, H. J. (1978) 'Adult Sexual Orientation and Attraction to Underage Persons', *Archives of Sexual Behaviour*, vol. 7, pp. 175–81.

Gunter, P. L. (1992) 'Social Work with Non-Traditional Families', in N. J. Woodman (ed), *Lesbian and Gay Lifestyles: A Guide for Counseling and Education*, New York: Irvington, pp. 87–110.

Hall, M. (1989) 'Private Experiences in the Public Domain: Lesbians in Organizations', in J. Hearn, D. L. Sheppard, P. Tancred-Sheriff and G. Burrell (ed.), *The Sexuality of Organization*, London: Sage, pp. 125–38.

Hanmer, J. and Statham, D. (1988) *Women and Social Work*, London: Macmillan.

Hanscombe, G. E. and Forster, J. (1982) *Rocking the Cradle: Lesbian Mothers. A Challenge in Family Living*, London: Sheba Feminist Publishers.

Hanvey, C. and Philpot, T. (eds) (1994) *Practising Social Work*, London: Routledge.

Hart, J. (1980) 'It's Just a Stage We're Going Through: The Sexual Politics of Casework', in M. Brake and R. Bailey (eds), *Radical Social Work and Practice*, London: Edward Arnold, pp. 43–63.

Hart, J. (1992) 'A Cocktail of Alarm: Same Sex Couples and Migration to Australia 1985–90', in K. Plummer (ed), *Modern Homosexualities*, London: Routledge.

Hart, J. and Richardson, D. (eds) (1981) *The Theory and Practice of Homosexuality*, London: Routledge & Kegan Paul.

Hawkins, P. and Shohet, R. (1989) *Supervision in the Helping Professions*, Milton Keynes: Open University Press.

Healey, E. and Mason, A. (eds) (1994) *Stonewall 25: The Making of the Lesbian and Gay Community in Britain*, London: Virago.

Hearn, K. (1991) 'Disabled Lesbians and Gays Are Here to Stay!', in T. Kaufmann and P. Lincoln (eds), *High Risk Lives*, Bridport: Prism Press, pp. 29–39.

Heathfield, M. (1988) 'The Youth Work Response to Lesbian and Gay Youth', *Youth and Policy*, vol. 23, pp. 19–22.

Hemmings, S. (1985) *A Wealth of Experience: The Lives of Older Women*, London: Pandora.

Hicks, S. (1996) 'The "Last Resort?" Lesbian and Gay Experiences of the Social Work Assessment Process in Fostering and Adoption', *Practice*, vol. 8, no. 2, pp. 15–24.

Hillin, A. (1985) 'When you Stop Hiding Your Sexuality', *Social Work Today*, vol. 4, pp. 18–19.

Hoeffer, B. (1981) 'Children's Acquisition of Sex-role Behaviour in Lesbian-Mother Familes', *American Journal of Orthopsychiatry*, vol. 5, pp. 536–44.

Home Office (1992a) *Gender and the Criminal Justice System*, London: Home Office.

Home Office (1992b) *Race and the Criminal Justice System*, London: Home Office.

Home Office, Department of Health and Welsh Office (1995) *National Standards for the Supervision of Offenders in the Community*, London: Home Office, Probation Training Division.

Howe, D. (1979) 'Agency, Function and Social Work Principles', *British Journal of Social Work*, vol. 9, no. 1, pp. 29–47.

Howe, D. (1986) 'The Segregation of Women and Their Work in the Personal Social Services', *Critical Social Policy*, vol. 5, no. 3, pp. 21–35.

Howe, D. (1987) *An Introduction to Social Work Theory*, Aldershot: Wildwood House.

Huggins, S.L. (1989) 'A Comparative Study of Self-Esteem of Adolescent Children of Divorced Lesbian Mothers and Divorced Heterosexual Mothers', in F. W. Bozett (ed), *Homosexuality and the Family*, New York: Harrington Park Press, pp. 123–35.

Hughes, B. and Mtezuka, M. (1992) 'Social work with older women: where have older women gone?', in M. Langan and L. Day (eds), *Women, Oppression and Social Work: Issues in Anti-Discriminatory Practice*, London: Routledge, pp. 220–41.

Husband, C. (1991) 'Race, Conflictual Politics, and Anti-Racist Social Work: Lessons from the Past for Action in the '90's', in C.D. Project Steering Group, *Setting the Context for Change*, Leeds: CCETSW, pp. 46–73.

Hutchinson-Reis, M. (1989) 'And for Those of Us Who Are Blacks? Black Politics in Social Work', in M. Langan and P. Lee (eds), *Radical Social Work Today*, London: Unwin Hyman, pp. 165–77.

Inner London Probation Service (1993) *Working With Difference*, London: ILPS.

Jeffrey-Poulter, S. (1991) *Peers, Queers and Commons: The Struggle for Gay Law Reform from 1950 to the Present*, London: Routledge.

Jones, B.M. and MacFarlane, K. (eds) (1980) *Sexual Abuse of Children: Selected Readings*, Washington, DC: National Center on Child Abuse and Neglect.

Jones, R. (1994) *Mental Health Act Manual*, London: Sweet & Maxwell.

Kaufmann, T. and Lincoln, P. (1991) *High Risk Lives: Lesbian and Gay Politics after the clause*, Bridport: Prism Press.

Kelly, J.J. (1977) 'The Ageing Male Homosexual', *American Journal of Orthopsychiatry*, vol. 43, no. 4, pp. 670–4.

Kent-Baguley, P. (1985) 'Is Being Gay Okay?', *Youth and Policy*, no. 14, autumn, pp. 16–21.

Kent-Baguley, P. (1990) 'Sexuality and Youth Work Practice', in T. Jeffs and M. Smith (eds), *Young People, Inequality and Youth Work*, London: Macmillan, pp. 99–119.

King, N. (1995) 'HIV and the Gay Male Community: One Clinician's Reflections Over the Years', in G. M. Herek and B. Greene (eds), *AIDS, Identity, and Community: The HIV Epidemic and Lesbians and Gay Men*, London: Sage, pp. 1–18.

Kirkpatrick, M., Smith, C., and Roy, R. (1981) 'Lesbian Mothers and Their Children: A Comparative Survey', *American Journal of Orthopsychiatry*, vol. 15, pp. 545–51.

Kitzinger, C. (1987) *The Social Construction of Lesbianism*, London: Sage.

Klein, C. (1990) 'Gay and Lesbian Counseling Centers: History and Function', in R. J. Kus (ed), *Keys to Caring: Assisting Your Gay and Lesbian Clients*, Boston: Alyson, pp. 312–20.

Kus, R. J. (ed.) (1990a) *Keys to Caring: Assisting Your Gay and Lesbian Clients*, Boston: Alyson.

Kus (1990b) 'Coming Out: Its Nature, Stage, and Health Concerns', in R. J. Kus (ed.), *Keys to Caring: assisting your Gay and Lesbian Clients*, Boston: Alyson, pp. 30–44.

Kus, R. J. (1990c) 'Alcoholism in the Gay and Lesbian Communities', in R. J. Kus (ed.), *Keys to Caring: Assisting Your Gay and Lesbian Clients*, Boston: Alyson, pp. 66–81.

Labour Campaign for Lesbian and Gay Rights (1986) *Legislation for Lesbian and Gay Rights: A Manifesto*, London: Labour Campaign for Lesbian and Gay Rights.

Labour Party (1992) *Labour Party Manifesto*, London: Labour Party.

Langan, M. and Day, L. (eds) (1992) *Women, Oppression and Social Work*, London: Routledge.

Langan, M. and Lee, P. (eds) (1989) *Radical Social Work Today*, London: Unwin Hyman.

Lloyd, M. (1993) 'Lesbian and Gay Clients and Residential Work', in C. McCaughey and K. Buckley (eds), *Sexuality, Youthwork and Probation Practice*, Sheffield: PAVIC Publications, pp. 37–48.

Logan, J., Kershaw, S., Karban, K., Mitts, S., Trotter, J. and Sinclair, M. (1996) *Confronting Prejudice: Lesbian and Gay Issues in Social Work Education*, Aldershot: Arena.

London Borough of Brent (1985) *A Child in Trust: Report of the Panel of Inquiry Investigating the Circumstances Surrounding the Death of Jasmine Beckford*, London: London Borough of Brent.

London Borough of Lambeth (1987) *Whose Child? The Report of the Panel Appointed to Inquire into the Death of Tyra Henry*, London: London Borough of Lambeth.

Lonsdale, S. (1990) *Women and Disability*, London: Macmillan.

Lovell, A. (1995) *When Your Child Comes Out*, London: Sheldon Press.

McCarthy, M. and Thompson, D. (1992) *Sex and the 3 R's. Rights, Responsibilities and Risks: A Sex Education Package for Working with People with Learning Difficulties*, Hove: Pavilion Press.

McCarthy, M. and Thompson, D. (1994) 'HIV/AIDS and safer sex work with people with learning disabilities', in A. Craft (ed.), *Sexuality and Learning Disabilities*, London: Routledge, pp. 186–201.

McCaughey, C. and Buckley, K. (1993) *Sexuality, Youth Work and Probation Practice*, Sheffield: Pavic Publications.

McIntosh, M. (1968) 'The Homosexual Role', *Social Problems*, vol. 16, no. 2, pp. 182–92.

McKenney, C. R. (1951) *Moral Problems in Social Work*, Milwaukee: Bruce Publishing Company.

Manning, M. (1988) 'The Implications of Clause 28', *Social Work Today*, 26 May 1988, pp. 14–15.

Margolies, L., Becker, M. and Jackson-Brewer, K. (1987) 'Internalised Homophobia: Identifying and Treating the Oppressor Within', in The Boston Lesbian Pyschologies Collective (eds) *Lesbian Psychologies: Explorations and Challenges*, Chicago: University of Illinois Press, pp. 229–41.

Martin, A. (1993) *The Guide to Lesbian and Gay Parenting*, London: Pandora.

Mason, A. (1994) 'The Scientific Baby and the Social Family: The Possibilities of Lesbian and Gay Parenting', in E. Healey and A. Mason (eds), *Stonewall 25*, London: Virago, pp. 137–49.

Mason-John, V. (ed.) (1995) *Talking Black: Lesbians of African and Asian Descent Speak Out*, London: Cassell.

Mason-John, V. and Khambatta. A. (1993) *Lesbians Talk Making Black Waves*, London: Scarlet Press.

May, T. (1991) *Probation: Politics, Policy and Practice*, Milton Keynes: Open University Press.

May, T. and Vass, A. A. (1996) *Working with Offenders: Issues, Contexts and Outcomes*, London: Sage.

Mayer, E. J. and Timms, N. (1970) *The Client Speaks*, London: Routledge & Kegan Paul.

Miller, B. (1979) 'Gay Fathers and Their Children', *Family Coordinator*, vol. 28, pp. 544–52.

Montsho, Q. (1995) 'Behind Locked Doors', in V. Mason-John (ed.), *Talking Black: Lesbians of African and Asian Descent Speak Out*, London: Cassell.

Morris, J. (ed.) (1989) *Able Lives: Women's Experiences of Paralysis*, London: The Women's Press.

Morris, J. (1993) 'Gender and Disability', in J. Swain, V. Finkelstein, S. French, and M. Oliver (eds), *Disabling Barriers – Enabling Environments*, London: Sage, pp. 85–92.

Munro, A. and McCulloch, W. (1969) *Psychiatry for Social Workers*, Oxford: Pergamon Press.

Munro, A., Manthei, B. and Small, J. (1989) *Counselling: The Skills of Problem Solving*, London: Routledge.

NACRO [National Association for the Care and Resettlement of Offenders] (1991) *A Fresh Start for Women Prisoners*, London: NACRO.

NAPO [National Association of Probation Officers] (1989) *Working with Lesbian and Gay Men as Clients of the Service: Good Practice Guidelines*, London: NAPO.

NAPO (1990) *Lesbian and Gay Rights – Challenging Heterosexism: A Training and Information Packet for Branches*, London: NAPO.

NATFHE (1986) [National Association of Teachers in Further and Higher Education] *Sexual Orientation: An Equal Opportunities Discussion Paper*,

London: National Association of Teachers in Further and Higher Education.

NATFHE (1993) *An Equal Opportunities Guide to Language*, London: National Association of Teachers in Further and Higher Education.

NATFHE (1994a) *Harrassment at Work: How to Deal with It*, London: National Association of Teachers in Further and Higher Education.

NATFHE (1994b) *A Best Practice Guide for Negotiations: Equal Opportunities*, London: National Association of Teachers in Further and Higher Education.

National Foster Care Association (1994) *Choosing to Foster: The Challenge to Care*, London: National Foster Care Association.

Nevins, P. (1991) 'The Making of a Radical Black Gay Man', in T. Kaufmann and P. Lincoln (eds), *High Risk Lives: Lesbian and Gay Politics after the Clause*, Bridport: Prism Press, pp. 93–108.

Nicoloff, L. K. and Stiglitz, E. A. (1987) 'Lesbian Alcoholism: Etiology, Treatment and Recovery', in Boston Lesbian Psychologies Collective (eds), *Lesbian Psychologies: Explorations and Challenges*, Chicago: University of Illinois Press, pp. 283–93.

O'Connor, N. and Ryan, R. (1993) *Wild Desires and Mistaken Identities*, London: Virago.

O'Hagan, K. (1986) *Crisis Intervention in Social Services*, London: Macmillan.

O'Hagan, K. (ed.) (1996) *Competence in Social Work Practice: A Practical Guide for Professionals*, London: Jessica Kingsley.

Oliver, M. (1983) *Social Work with Disabled People*, London: Macmillan.

Oliver, M. (ed.) (1991) *Social Work, Disabled People and Disabling Environments*, London: Jessica Kingsley.

Oliver, M. and Barnes, C. (1993) 'Discrimination, Disability and Welfare: From Needs to Rights', in J. Swain, V. Finkelstein, S. French and M. Oliver (eds), *Disabling Barriers – Enabling Environments*, London: Sage, pp. 267–77.

Osler, A. (1995) *Introduction to the Probation Service*, Winchester: Waterside Press.

O'Sullivan, S. and Parmer, P. (1992) *Lesbians Talk Safer Sex*, London: Scarlet Press.

O'Sullivan, J. (1991) 'Psychologists Undecided on Need for Father', *The Independent*, 12th March 1991, p. 3.

Øvretveit, J. (1993) *Coordinating Community Care: Multidisciplinary Teams and Care Management*, Buckingham: Open University Press.

Padel, U. (1995) 'HIV, AIDS and Probation Practice', in Williams, B. (ed.), *Probation Values*, Birmingham: Venture Press, pp. 155–70.

Palmer, A. (1995) 'Lesbian and Gay Rights Campaigning: A Report from the Coalface', in A. R. Wilson (ed.), *A Simple Matter of Justice?*, London: Cassell, pp. 32–50.

Parkin, W. (1989) 'Private Experiences in the Public Domain: Sexuality and Residential Care Organisations', in J. Hearn, D. L. Sheppard, P. Tancred-Sheriff and G. Burrell (eds), *The Sexuality of Organization*, London: Sage, pp. 110–24.

Parton, C. and Parton, N. (1988), 'Women, the Family and Child Protection', *Critical Social Policy*, vol. 24, no. 8, pp. 38–49.

Patterson, C. J. (1992) 'Children of Lesbian and Gay Parents', *Child Development*, vol. 63, pp. 1025–42.

Patterson, C. J. (1994) 'Children of the Lesbian Baby Boom: Behavioural Adjustment, Self-concepts, and Sex Role Identity', in B. Greene and G. M. Herek (eds), *Lesbian and Gay Psychology: Theory, Research, and Clinical Applications*, London: Sage, pp. 156–75.

Payne, M. (1991) *Modern Social Work Theory: A Critical Introduction*. London: Macmillan.

Payne, M. (1992) 'Psychodynamic Theory within the Politics of Social Work Theory', *Journal of Social Work Practice*, vol. 6, no. 2, pp. 141–9.

Pearce, J. J. (1996) 'The Values of Social Work', in A. A. Vass (ed), *Social Work Competences: Core Knowledge, Values and Skills*, London: Sage, pp. 36–61.

Pearson, G., Treseder, J., and Yelloly, M. (1988) *Social Work and the Legacy of Freud*, London: Macmillan.

Pedersen, P. B., Draguns, J. G., Louner, W. J. and Trimble, J. E. (eds) (1989) *Counseling Across Cultures*, 3rd edn, Honolulu: University of Hawaii Press.

Perelberg, R. J. and Miller, C. A. (1990) *Gender and Power in Families*, London: Routledge.

Pierce, D. (1992) 'Policies of Concern for Practice with Lesbian Women and Gay Men', in N. J. Woodman (ed), *Lesbian and Gay Lifestyles: A Guide For Counseling and Education*, New York: Irvington, pp. 171–90.

Pilalis, J. and Anderton, J. (1986) 'Feminism and Family Therapy – A Possible Meeting Point', *Journal of Family Therapy*, vol. 9, no. 2, pp. 99–113.

Pincus, L. (ed.) (1953) *Social Casework in Marital Problems*, London: Tavistock Publications.

Plummer, K. (1975) *Sexual Stigma: An Interactionist Account*, London: Routledge & Kegan Paul.

Plummer, K. (1992) *Modern Homosexualities*, London: Routledge.

Pollack, S. and Vaughn, J. (eds) (1987) *Politics of the Heart: A Lesbian Parenting Anthology*, New York: Firebrand Books.

Probation Training Unit, Home Office (1994) *Introducing competences*, London: Home Office.

Radford, J. and Cobley, J. (1987) 'Lesbian Custody Projects and Social Work Reports', *Rights of Women Bulletin*, May.

Rafkin, L. (1990) *Different Mothers: Sons and Daughters of Lesbians Talk about Their Lives*, Pittsburgh: Cleis Press.

Rayner, E. (1986) *Human Development: An Introduction to the Psychodynamics of Growth, Maturity, and Ageing*, 3rd edn, London: Routledge.

Raynor, P., Smith, D. and Vanstone, M. (1994) *Effective Probation Practice*, London: Macmillan.

Rights of Women Lesbian Custody Group (1986) *Lesbian Mother's Legal Handbook*, London: The Women's Press.

Robertson, R. (1981) 'Young Gays', in J. Hart and D. Richardson (eds), *The Theory and Practice of Homosexuality*, London: Routledge & Kegan Paul. pp. 170–6.

Roelofs, S. (1991) 'Labour and the Natural Order: Intentionally Promoting

Heterosexuality', in T. Kaufmann and L. Lincoln, *High Risk Lives*, Bridport: Prism Press. pp. 179–98.

Rofes, E. E. (1990) 'Notes on Suicide and Suicidal Ideation Among Gays and Lesbians', in R. J. Kus (ed), *Keys to Caring: Assisting Your Gay and Lesbian Clients*, Boston: Alyson, pp. 99–105.

Romans, P. (1992) 'Daring to Pretend? Motherhood and Lesbianism', in K. Plummer, *Modern Homosexualities*, London: Routledge. pp. 98–107.

ROW Policy and Lesbian Custody Groups (1988) 'Outlawing the Lesbian Community: Clause 27', *Rights of Women Bulletin*, London: Rights of Women.

Ryan, J. with Thomas, F. (1987) *The Politics of Mental Handicap*, revised edn, London: Free Association Books.

Sable, R. (1990) 'Gay and Lesbian Prisoners', in R. J. Kus (ed.), *Keys to Caring: Assisting Your Gay and Lesbian Clients*, Boston: Alyson Publications, pp. 182–92.

Saffron, L. (1994) *Challenging Conceptions: Planning a Family by Self-Insemination*, London: Cassell.

Saffron, L. (1996) *What About the Children: Sons and Daughters of Lesbian and Gay Parents Talk About Their Lives*, London: Cassell.

Sage, A. (1991) 'Can Gay Couples Be Good Parents?', *The Independent on Sunday*, 10 March 1991, p. 23.

Sanderson, T. (1995) *Mediawatch: The Treatment of Male and Female Homosexuality in the British Media*, London: Cassell.

Sarafino, E. P. (1979) 'An Estimate of Nationwide Incidence of Sexual Offences Against Children', *Child Welfare*, vol. 58, pp. 127–34.

Segal, L. (1994) *Straight Sex: The Politics of Pleasure*, London: Virago.

Seneviratne, S. (1995) '. . . and Some of Us Are Older', in V. Mason-John (ed.), *Talking Black: Lesbians of African and Asian Descent Speak Out*, London: Cassell, pp. 108–29.

Senior, P. and Woodhill, D. (1992) *Gender, Crime and Probation Practice*, Sheffield: PAVIC Publications.

Sheldon, B. (1978) 'Theory and Practice in Social Work: A Re-Examination of a Tenuous Relationship', *British Journal of Social Work*, vol. 8, no. 1, pp. 1–22.

Shildo, A. (1994) 'Internalised Homophobia: Conceptual and Empirical Issues in Measurement', in B. Greene and G. M. Herek (eds), *Lesbian and Gay Psychology: Theory, Research and Clinical Applications*, London: Sage, pp. 176–205.

Skeates, J. and Jabri, J. (eds) (1988) *Fostering and Adoption by Lesbians and Gay Men*, London: Strategy Unit.

Smale, G. and Tusan, G. with Biehal, N. and Marsh, P. (1993) *Empowerment, Assessment, Care Management and the Skilled Worker*, London: HMSO.

Smart, C. (1995) *Law, Crime and Sexuality: Essays in Feminism*, London: Sage.

Smith, A. M. (1992) 'Resisting the Erasure of Lesbian Sexuality: A Challenge for Queer Activism', in K. Plummer (ed.) *Modern Homosexualities*, London: Routledge, pp. 200–16.

Smith, D. (1995) 'The Anatomy of a Campaign', in A. R. Wilson (ed.), *A Simple Matter of Justice?*, London: Cassell, pp. 10–31.

Smyth, C. (1992) *Lesbians Talk Queer Notions*, London: Scarlet Press.

Statham, D. (1978) *Radicals in Social Work*, London: Routledge & Kegan Paul.

Statham, R. and Whitehead, P. (eds) (1992) *Managing the Probation Service. Issues for the 1990s*, Harlow: Longman.

Stewart, W. (1995) *Cassell's Queer Companion*, London: Cassell.

Streetwatch Implementation Advisory Committee (1994) *Final Report of the Streetwatch Implementation Advisory Committee*, Sydney: Anti-Discrimination Board of New South Wales.

Streetwise Youth (1995) *Streetwise Youth Information Sheet*, London: Streetwise

Strommen, E. (1990) 'Hidden Branches and Growing Pains: Homosexuality and the Family Tree', in F. W. Bozett and M. B. Sussman (eds), *Homosexuality and Family Relations*, New York: Harrington Park Press, pp. 9–34.

Stuart, O. (1993) 'Double Oppression: An Appropriate Starting Point?', in J. Swain, V. Finkelstein, S. French and M. Oliver (eds), *Disabling Barriers – Enabling Environments*, London: Sage, pp. 93–100.

Studzinski, K. (1994) *Lesbians Talk Left Politics*, London: Scarlet Press.

Suriyaprakasam, S. (1995) 'Some of Us Are Younger', in V. Mason-John (ed.), *Talking Black: Lesbians of African and Asian Descent Speak Out*, London: Cassell, pp. 94–107.

Tasker, F. and Golombok, S. (1991) 'Children Raised by Lesbian Mothers – The Empirical Evidence', *Family Law*, pp. 184–7.

Tasker, F. and Golombok, S. (1995) 'Adults Raised as Children in Lesbian Families', *American Journal of Orthopsychiatry*, vol. 65, no. '2, pp. 203–15.

Tatchell, P. (1992) 'Equal Rights for All: Strategies for Lesbian and Gay Equality in Britian', in K. Plummer (ed.), *Modern Homosexualities*, London: Routledge, pp. 237–48.

Thompson, D. (1994) 'Sexual Experience and Sexual Identity for Men with Learning Difficulties Who Have Sex with Men', *Changes: An International Journal of Psychology and Psychotherapy*, vol. 12, no. 4, pp. 254–63.

Thompson, M. (1993) *Anti-discriminatory Practice*, London: Macmillan.

Tievsky, D. L. (1988) 'Homosexual Clients and Homophobic Social Workers', *Journal of Independent Social Work,* vol. 2 no. 3, pp. 51–62.

Tobin, A. (1990) 'Lesbianism and the Labour Party: The GLC experience', *Feminist Review*, 34, pp. 56–66.

Trenchard, L. and Warren, H. (1984) *Something to tell you*, London: London Gay Teenage Group.

Trenchard, L. and Warren, H. (1985) *Talking about Youth Work*, London: London Teenage Group.

Tully, C. (1992) 'Research on Older Lesbian Women: What Is Known, What Is Not Known, and How to Learn More', in N. J. Woodman (ed.), *Lesbian and Gay Lifestyles: A guide for Counseling and Education*, New York: Irvington, pp. 235–65.

Turk, V. and Brown, H. (1992) 'Sexual abuse and adults with learning disabilities', *Mental Handicap*, vol. 20, no. 2, pp. 56–8.

UNISON (trade union) (1995) *Double Jeopardy: A Lobbying Pamphlet for Lesbian and Gay Equality Under Immigration Laws*, London: Unison/Stonewall Immigration Group.

Vass, A. A. (1990) *Alternatives To Prison*, London: Sage.

Wakling, L. and Bradstock, M. (eds) (1995) *Beyond Blood: Writings on the Lesbian and Gay Family*, Sydney: Blackwattle Press.

Walker, H. and Beaumont, B. (1981) *Probation Work: Critical Theory and Socialist Practice*, Oxford: Blackwell.

Walker, H. and Beaumont, B. (eds) (1985) *Working with Offenders*, London: Macmillan.

Watney, S. (1994) 'Numbers and Nightmares: HIV/AIDS in Britain', in E. Healey and A. Mason (eds), *Stonewall 25: The Making of the Lesbian and Gay Community in Britain*, London: Virago, pp. 150–66.

Weeks, J. (1981) 'The Problems of Older Homosexuals', in J. Hart and D. Richardson (eds), *The Theory and Practice of Homosexuality*, London: Routledge & Kegan Paul, pp. 177–84.

Weeks, J. (1991) *Against Nature: Essays on History, Sexuality and Identity*, London: Rivers Oram.

Weeks, J. (1995) *Invented Moralities: Sexual Values In An Age Of Uncertainty*, Cambridge: Polity Press.

Weir, A. (1974) 'The Family, Social Work and the Welfare State', in S. Allen, L. Sanders and J. Wallis (eds), *Conditions of Illusion*, Leeds: Feminist Books, pp. 217–28.

Wertheimer, A. (1987) 'Mourning in Secret', *New Society*, vol. 80, no. 1268, pp. 8–9.

Whitfield, R. (1991) 'Don't Give In to Pressure', *Community Care*, No. 848, p. 16.

Williams, B. (ed.) (1995) *Probation Values*, Birmingham: Venture Press.

Wilson, A. R. (ed) (1995) *A Simple Matter of Justice?*, London: Cassell.

Wilson, E. (1977) *Women and the Welfare State*, London: Tavistock.

Winnicott, D. W. (1986) *Home Is Where We Start From*, London: Penguin.

Winnicott, D. W. (1988) *Babies and Their Mothers*, London: Free Association Books.

Woodman, N. J. (ed) (1992) *Lesbian and Gay Lifestyles: A Guide for Counseling and Education*, New York: Irvington Publishers.

World Health Organisation (1978) *The ICD-9 Classification of Mental and Behavioural Disorders: Clinical Descriptions and Diagnostic Guidelines*, Geneva: WHO.

Worrall, A. (1990) *Offending Women*, London: Routledge.

Worrall, A. (1995) 'Equal Opportunity or Equal Disillusion? The Probation Service and Anti-Discriminatory Practice', in B. Williams (ed.), *Probation Values*, Birmingham: Ventura Press, pp. 29–46.

Yelloly, M. (1980) *Social Work Theory and Psychoanalysis*, London: Van Nostrand Reinhold.

Younghusband, E. (1959) *Report of the Working Party on the Local Authority Health and Welfare Sevices*, London: HMSO.

Zarb, G. (1991) Creating a Supportive Environment: Meeting the Needs of People who are Ageing with a Disability', in M. Oliver (ed.) *Social Work: Disabled People and Disabling Environments*, London: Jessica Kingsley Publishers, pp. 177–203.

Ziebold, T. O. and Mongeon, J. E. (1985) *Gay and Sober, Directions for Counselling and Therapy*, New York: Harrington Park Press.

Author Index

Subject Index